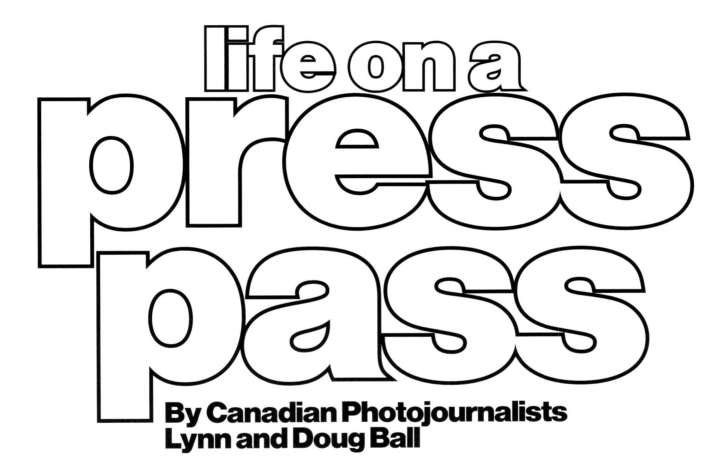

life on a press pass

By Canadian Photojournalists Lynn and Doug Ball

life on a
press pass
By Canadian Photojournalists
Lynn and Doug Ball

ISBN 0-9688255-4-0

Wallbridge House Publishing
Belleville, Ontario, Canada
K8N 3N9
www.littlebrickbookhouse.com

First printing 2005

Editorial team: Project director, Orland French; Editor and Marketer, Janice Middleton; Writers and Photographers, Lynn and Doug Ball

Layout and design: Jozef VanVeenen, tikit visuals, Trenton, Ontario

Thanks to Loyalist College of Belleville for providing facilities for our planning sessions.

Life on a Press Pass was funded entirely by investments from generous individuals in the private sector. They believed in preserving Canadian history as recorded by Lynn and Doug Ball. Many thanks to them for their faith.

Printed and bound in Canada by
Friesens Corporation
Altona, Manitoba
R0G 0B0
Canada

From Father to Sons

*Lynn, left, and Doug, right, tower over their father John at Ottawa International Airport.
John Ball had been an air force photographer.*

"Their late father Johnny, a capable photographer and an amateur athlete, once
said to me many years ago that he wished Lynn would get more involved in sports
as Doug was doing. Sometime later he also said that he wished Doug would forget
about sports and get involved with a camera as Lynn was doing."
– *Ivor Williams, former managing editor, The London Free Press*

'Don't show it unless it's the best'

By Lynn Ball

Vicki Govan

When I was a kid in the late 1940s, growing up in London, Ont., I thought every house had a darkroom. I would look for the darkroom in other people's houses and then I'd ask where their darkroom was.

Learning photography from my father at home was better than school. A perfectionist, he made sure everything I did was to the best of my ability. The first time I made 8X10-inch prints he asked to see them. Someone was paying me for these. He asked me what was wrong with the prints I'd made. I told him and then he ripped them up, sending me back to the darkroom saying, "Don't show anything to anybody unless it is the best." It was a lesson that I understood and he was right.

In his later years, my father told me that the enlarger I learned to make prints on was "liberated" from Karl Doenitz's house at the end of the Second World War. Doenitz ran the German navy and U-boats and negotiated Germany's final surrender.

I was interested in sports cars and started photographing races for U.S. magazines. And with the help of Ivor Williams, our neighbour and the managing editor of *The London Free Press*, I got a job as a copy boy at the newspaper. Ivor and my father were both Second World War vets and we lived in a VLA (Veterans' Land Administration) subdivision. Ivor was a fighter pilot flying Spitfires and Mustangs. My father, John, was a sergeant major, a photographer in air reconnaissance.

I was covering a car race at Harewood Acres near London when I took a series of pictures with my Rolleiflex of a driver jumping from his racecar that had blown a radiator hose. He was soaked with scalding water and pulled his pants down as he ran from the car. *The Free Press* ran the four-picture sequence on Page One. The pictures were picked up by *The Canadian Press* news co-op and then moved worldwide on *The Associated Press* wire. The Driver With His Pants Down won the *CP* picture of the month award.

With this in hand and Ivor's recommendation, I got a job as a darkroom technician with *Canadian Press* in Toronto and I was able to freelance for the news co-operative as well as do darkroom work. I shot the Beatles' first Canadian tour, NHL hockey, including the 1964 Stanley Cup, movie stars Elizabeth Taylor and Richard Burton, and the 1964 Royal visit by Queen Elizabeth II and Prince Philip. I was paid the princely sum of $5 for every picture used. No pay if nothing used was a great incentive to give the editors quality pictures that made the wire.

In August 1965, Gil Purcell, *CP* general manager, assigned me to Ottawa as the news co-operative's first national photographer. It turned out to be very successful. Purcell was happy and a year later

> I would like to dedicate this book to my late mother and father, Alice and John Ball, who persevered to make sure I was on the right track, and to my daughter Fiona.
> – Lynn Ball

Chuck Mitchell, who worked in the darkroom in Toronto as well, was assigned to Ottawa as a photographer. Chuck and I worked very hard and there was never a reason why we couldn't get a picture, just ask our photo editor Stan Mulcahy. Sometimes we were arrested or detained by the police. And on at least one occasion, I palmed the roll and substituted a blank one when police confiscated the film. Several times Stan thought we would all go to jail.

We had no real work schedules, working when we were needed. Many times I drove to London on days off only to find I had to hop back in the car and race back to Ottawa to cover something. No cell phones then.

I left *CP* in 1967 and freelanced, then did a one-year stint at The National Research Council before heading off in January 1969 on a boat to Australia with brother Doug and my 1962 Corvette. It ended up being a three-year round the world trip.

Our travel costs were covered by a series of jobs. In Australia, I worked as a photographer for a chain of small newspapers. In Barcelona, I was an offset photo engraver during the day and a cook at night in a British pub called Leon Rojo owned by an American. Then I left Spain for the United Kingdom where a photo exhibit on urban renewal I did for the City of Glasgow got great reviews and led to a job with the Scottish Tourist Board where I also ran its photo department.

British Prime Minister Ted Heath opened the Glasgow show. I was giving him a tour of some of the exhibit when he noticed the small Canadian flag on my lapel. He said to me, "What is a Canadian doing in Glasgow?" "I guess you could call it a little foreign aid," I replied. Heath wasn't amused.

I left Scotland and came back to Canada to be chief photographer for *The Ottawa Citizen*. *Canadian Press* had a contract to do the photography for *the Citizen* and *CP's* photo editor Stan Mulcahy offered me the job to start Jan. 1, 1972. *The Citizen* took control of their photo staff in November 1973 and I stayed on with the newspaper. When we moved to a new plant with an offset printing press, *The Citizen* became the largest offset newspaper in the world. It was cutting-edge technology that meant colour pictures in the newspaper every day.

It was exciting and challenging to cover events in colour. I carried 35 mm Nikon cameras for black and white and 2 1/4 Hasselblads for colour. I felt like a packhorse carrying all this equipment. It was soon realized that 35 mm colour negs were just as good in newsprint and the job became a lot easier.

The Citizen was a very proud newspaper and liked having its own pictures in colour. News events took me to many places just so we could have our own original photographs.

The next big change was the switch to digital photography. Digital cameras have really improved over the few years they have been around. It is almost point and shoot now. I have had young photographers who have never used film cameras ask me, "What was it like to take pictures when you had to focus?"

I stayed with *The Citizen* as chief photographer until I retired in August 2003.

The Power, The Glory and the Sundance Kid

By Doug Ball

Phil Ferrari

We had a darkroom in our home when I was growing up in the '40s and '50s but I didn't care that much as I was too busy playing hockey and baseball.

Near the end of high school I started learning a bit about photography from Dad and got a part-time job in the camera department of Sayvette's in London. One day, store manager Pat Quinn asked me to take some pictures of a rock group he'd brought in to play at Treasure Island Gardens. They were The Rolling Stones and I spent about an hour in their dressing room mostly talking to Charlie Watts about photography.

Brother Lynn was working for *The Canadian Press* in Ottawa so I packed my bags and headed northeast. Using his name, I got my first assignment from *United Press International* Ottawa boss Gary Bartlett, a terrific, gentle man.

In early 1967, Lynn left *CP* and they chose me to replace him, which was a very tough row to hoe. After several months in Ottawa covering visits by world leaders during our Centennial year, I was demoted to the darkroom in Toronto to learn more about photography.

I worked at *CP* until January 1969, when Lynn and I took off in his 1962 Corvette, first to Australia and eventually around the world. I got a job in the darkroom at *The Melbourne Herald-Sun* and had to lend my brother $20 to start his job at a small newspaper chain 90 miles out of Melbourne.

We saved enough for a two-month tour of Australia, a month in South Africa and on to Europe. I worked as a labourer and bartender at the Old Smuggler's Inn in Jersey, Channel Islands, all of 1970 until I earned enough money to make it home after being away nearly two years.

Back in Ottawa, I got work with Dominion Wide Photos which handled pictures for *The Ottawa Journal*. A short time later, *Canadian Press* took over *The Journal* contract and they didn't want to hire me back. Thanks to *Journal* Managing Editor Bill Metcalfe, who talked *CP Picture* Editor Mel Sufrin into taking me back on a three-month trial. *CP Photo* was in my blood.

I left *CP-Journal* in the fall of 1972 and after Christmas and New Years in the Canary Islands, I returned to France and played hockey, defence, for the City of Caen, Normandy. I learned some French and drank some fine wine.

CP, needing a photographer in Montreal for the upcoming Olympics in 1976, wrote and asked if I would like the job. I was thrilled. It was the best of times. I met my wife Gail, worked with Lynn covering the Olympics and worked with two of the greatest guys, Chuck Stoody and Chris Haney. They called us "The Power, The Glory and the Sundance Kid." The

Power was Chris as photo editor. I was The Glory for winning a couple of awards and Chuck was ... Chuck!!

It was the absolute highlight of my times in photography. There was never a schedule to follow; we worked when there was news and loved it. Many times my breakfast was steamed hotdogs at the Montreal Forum just before a Habs game or a #3 roast beef at Magnon's Tavern in the Point.

In 1984, after Nick was born, a brother to Gordie, I left *CP* and went to *The Montreal Gazette* as photo editor. I had left my comfort zone. It turned out to be the worst job I've ever had. The editors treated me like shit and the photographers did the same. For example, one photographer, Richard Arless, wrote on my goodbye card, "Fuck Off, Doug."

Back in late 1979, Chris Haney had invented a board game called *Trivial Pursuit* and we had been talking about building a golf course near Toronto. He called me at the photo desk in late July 1987, and said, "Does today seem like a good day to quit?"

I said, "You're damn right!", hung up ... and quit.

Chris, along with buddy Scott Abbott, let me help them build Devil's Pulpit and Devil's Paintbrush golf courses.

In 1999, I went back to freelancing corporate events, which I enjoy. It's nice to see boys Gordie and Nick doing well and also doing a little photography. Their grandpa would be proud.

Doug and Lynn show off their wedding finery as they prepare to cover the marriage of Prince Andrew and Sarah Ferguson, in July 1986. London cabbie Danny Doyle snapped this photo of the brothers at work.

True Masters of Their Craft

By Marc Garneau, Canadian astronaut

Like most people who pick up a newspaper, my eye is first drawn to the picture, then to the headline and then to the text. Most of the time, the photograph is mundane and totally forgettable. Occasionally, it grabs my attention like a vise and is never forgotten. In some cases, it is the story and nothing else need be said.

Every assignment given to news photographers Doug and Lynn Ball has carried with it the promise, however remote, that an unforgettable picture could be taken, a picture that would say it all and even ultimately define a moment or even a period in our history. This book contains such photographs, images around which whole essays can be written because they are now part of the social or political history of our country.

But let's be clear on the process. News photographers don't just show up politely on request, position themselves for the shot and go click. Great pictures rarely occur in such circumstances. For that to happen, the news photographer requires a mind of his own, a certain disrespect for convention and in some cases, for the law, a lightning quick ability to assess the situation in terms of the desired frame, the lighting conditions, the amount of movement, the willingness of the subject and finally, a precise knowledge of what his camera can deliver. When everything falls into place, and it rarely does, the result is unforgettable.

Doug and Lynn Ball have been chronicling the history of Canada through their photography for the past four decades. I had the pleasure of meeting Lynn in 1984 when he covered my first launch and provided me with a memento I will always cherish, a photograph of Space Shuttle Challenger as it lifted off at dawn from pad 39B at the Kennedy Space Center. What made it special for me was that it had been taken by a fellow Canadian, a news photographer sent down by *The Ottawa Citizen* to cover my story. It was also a damn good picture taken in very difficult lighting conditions. A rising Shuttle is as bright as the sun.

This book presents many indelible images, some of which are truly familiar to people of my generation. They evoke the times through which we as Canadians journeyed as we rode into the 1960s with growing momentum and a strong desire to define ourselves in our own terms. From the local arena to the national or international stage, these photographs resurrect a flood of memories, of the events themselves, or of the surrounding personal context of our lives at that time. They are evocative triggers that give us a perspective on our own personal journeys.

I confess a strong admiration for news photographers, not only as superb technicians of their craft but also because of their ability to sense the moment, the opportunity, the importance of something which is actually still in the future when they decide to act. That premonition and that ability to detach themselves from the rest of us who are living the moment, in order to record it, is a skill given to few. Doug and Lynn Ball have mastered their craft.

Away Back in the Middle Ages

By Orland French, Project Director

Luke Hendry

A few years ago I was entertaining a class of journalism students by explaining how a linotype machine works. They looked at me as if I were an alchemist out of the Middle Ages. What do you mean, you melted down lead and moulded little letters from it? How did you survive the noxious lead fumes poisoning the air? Is that why you have no hair?

Here we have a book in which photographers entertain us with tales of taking pictures on some obsolete medium called film. They tell us they broke speed limits hustling that film back to the newsroom, or entrusted it to Air Canada to deliver on the next flight, or processed it themselves in a makeshift washroom lab on a swaying, lurching railway car.

That was not the Middle Ages, kids. It happened in our lifetime! Now that we're in the Digital Age of Point'n'Shoot, we snap a hundred images and zap them back to the newsroom by satellite, hoping one of the hundred is usable. And the young photographers ask the old geezers, "What was it like in the days when you had to focus?"

Well, sonny, there were two rules: F8 and Be There. Now that everything is automatic and you don't need to know your F8 from your JPEG, the paramount rule is Be There. Anticipate, create, innovate, and get yourself a good picture. The Ball Brothers got great pictures the way Wayne Gretzky got so many goals: they knew where to be. And, like Gordie Howe, sometimes they elbowed a few rules out of the way to get a good shot. As you will see, anticipation and innovation led to many of the memorable news pictures found in *Life on a Press Pass*.

Working on this book was a huge amount of fun mixed with anxiety and trepidation. The word "scamps" often came to mind and I realized why their boss Stan Mulcahy at *Canadian Press* thought they would all wind up in jail.

Enjoy the book. It's all true, I'm sure.

I Call It Serendipity

By Janice Middleton, Editor/Marketer

Doug Ball

One splendid afternoon in the fall of 2003, I was browsing through the shops in Merrickville when I spotted a large photograph of the Beatles signed by Lynn Ball. "I know that guy," I said to the shop owner. At this point I hadn't seen Lynn in many years, since our *Ottawa Citizen* days. I called him and we got together. Looking through his photos and listening to his stories, I said, "The Ball brothers should do a book." That's when Lynn showed me the binder he had created with just that in mind, a pretty good start. Serendipity. So we got to work and here we are. We had a lot of fun doing this project and it brought back newsroom memories. I hope you like it too.

Table of Contents

We Got By with a Little Help from Our Friends

Thanks to Ivor Williams, former managing editor of *The London Free Press*, for giving me the start. To *The Ottawa Citizen* and *The Canadian Press* for allowing me to express myself while working and for allowing the use of photos in this book. To Frank Lennon, photographer at *The Toronto Star*, for helping me out when I first moved to Toronto. Thanks to my photo editors Stan Mulcahy, Bill Rose, Alge Kaminga, Richard Starnes, Mike Gillespie, Drew Gragg and Johnny Major, I know I gave you some grey hair. To Julian Riches for scanning all those old dirty negatives. To Bruno Schlumberger for shooting the cover picture. A very special thank you to *Citizen* librarian Liisa Touminen, a wonderful person, for helping me find countless stories, dates and photos. To Victoria Govan for putting up with my late nights of writing and hours on the computer. To the investors who had enough faith in us to finance this book.

A thank you to all my fellow photographers. We helped each other and enjoyed our times together. There was nothing like a Royal Tour or Olympic Games in Canada to get us all together. I'll try to name them but I know I'll leave some out: Chuck Mitchell, Wayne Cuddington, the late Malak, Rod MacIvor, Boris Spremo, Chris Mikula, Wayne Hiebert, Pat McGrath, Ted Church, Al Cave, Jean

●

TO THOSE WHO BELIEVED IN US

THANKS TO THE FOLLOWING INVESTORS WHO DISPLAYED THE COURAGE AND GOOD FAITH TO PRESERVE THIS SLICE OF CANADIAN PHOTOJOURNALISM

SCOTT ABBOTT
DOUGLAS BUMSTEAD
JEFFREY AND KIMBERLY CAMERON
ROGER AND GLENDA COOKE
VICTORIA GOVAN
CHRIS HANEY
RONALD HOPPER
J. T. MURPHY
DR. JOHN TOBIN

●

Levac, Hans Deryk, Dick Loek, Norm Betts, Hugh Wesley, Ted Grant, Scott Grant, Ian MacAlpine, Chris Swartz, Morris Lamont, Sam McLeod, Bill Ironsides, Barry Gray, Mike Pinder, Larry MacDougal, Lawrence Lee, Tim O'Lett, Ron Poling, Bryce Flynn, Fred Chartrand, Andrew Vaughn, Jim Young, Denis Paquin, Spud, Andy Clarke, Tom Hanson, Graham Bezant, Paul Vathis, Jack Thornell, Peter Bregg and Terry Hancey. And of course Janice Middleton for pushing me to restart this project.
– *Lynn Ball*

I would like to thank the following people for all those good things that happened ... and when you read your name, I hope you will remember when and why; because I do:

Gary and Red, Gary Bartlett, Stan Mulcahy, Mel Sufrin, Harold Herschell, Fred Blyth, Mr. and Mrs. Warren, Bill Metcalfe, Joey Slinger, Armand Demma, Chris Haney, Chuck Stoody, Scott Abbott, Jean Fiset, Clair Perry, Jacques Boissinot, George Cree, Little Horn, Bernard Brault, Mel Morris, Dave Caulkin, Ian Stewart, Peter Brosseau, Brad Henderson, Doug Holland, Ron Poling, Michael Principe, David Burman, Bill Hewitt and HRH The Prince of Wales.
– *Doug Ball*

Why We Drove Madly Through Snowstorms To Deliver Film by Hand

In the digital age it is difficult to imagine why films had to be physically transported back to the printing plant, sometimes at great speed. Why not just send them by wire? Here's why.

When *The Citizen* moved to its present plant on Baxter Road in Ottawa in 1973 it installed an offset printing press. This made it feasible to run colour news pictures instead of black and white. It was great for local pictures but out-of-town wirephoto colour was of very poor quality. When colour was to be sent on the wire a colour print had to be made. Then the print had to be transmitted three times through colour filters, one time for each of the three primary colours – red, blue and yellow. The transmitter changed the image into sound which was transmitted over telephone lines. At *The Citizen*

the receiver changed the sound back into an image. Any noise on the telephone line made patterns or fuzziness on the final image.

All three of these colour images had to line up perfectly. If they didn't, they were off-register and the colour inks didn't match up, resulting in a fuzzy or misaligned picture. The pictures were very seldom even acceptable. *The Citizen* needed the original film delivered back to Ottawa in time for deadline so we would have the latest news photos plus the best quality available. This put the pressure on me not only to shoot news events in colour but to get it back to *The Citizen* before deadline. We succeeded. Today, in the digital age, colour pictures being sent back to the paper are flawless.
– *Lynn Ball*

These guys were lucky all the time

Lynn and Doug Ball are well known to those who work in the media. What their colleagues have to say is highly complimentary, mostly.

Lynn and Doug Ball were diplomatic on assignment but also aggressive when required and always came back with the picture – not always the picture that I would envision, but with images that were most often far better than I had anticipated. The stories in this book describe some of the difficulties and the lengths to which they often had to go to get that picture. I can attest that all of these stories are true without embellishment.

There were some trying times of course, like the days an Ottawa police sergeant would walk into my office to dump a pile of parking tickets for our rented staff cars on my desk. And then there was that repetitive plea from the Governor-General's assistant press secretary, Madeleine d'Auray, when calling to tell me of a photo opportunity at Government House, "...and whoever you are sending, Stan, will you please make sure they wear socks."
– *Stan Mulcahy, former photo editor, The Canadian Press*

When Doug and I worked together the opposition would always say Doug was "lucky " all the time. Well, when you're "lucky" all the time, it means you're good !
– *Chris Haney, photographer, photo editor and co-inventor of Trivial Pursuit*

Whenever something interesting, significant or simply bizarre happened in Canadian politics, the Ball brothers were there. Thank goodness for that.
– *Charles Gordon, writer*

Doug and Lynn Ball's work represents the highest standards of Canadian photojournalism. The two combine a passion for both life and their craft that is reflected in their photos. Wherever the action was, you were bound to find one of them shooting away.
– *John Honderich, former publisher, Toronto Star*

I first met Lynn 30 years ago at *The Ottawa Citizen* and have consistently marveled at his professional and creative ability to capture the moment on film and disc. Lynn and Doug have combined their years of photographic excellence to bring readers some of their finest work in a beautiful book. They have built an international reputation by demonstrating an insatiable appetite for identifying something unique that resonates immediately with appreciative readers.
– *Jim Orban, publisher, The Ottawa Citizen*

Journalists have always known that the Ball brothers were at the top of their craft. In this unique book, we not only see their marvellous take on Canadian history; we now learn the stories behind the images. Truly a feast for the eyes!
– *Mike Duffy, CTV News, Ottawa*

I was a junior photographer at *The Ottawa Citizen* in the summer of 1981 when Lynn, then chief photographer, gave me an opportunity to get my feet wet in the business. I envied Lynn's job, as I did Doug's, as a staff photographer. Their assignments took them to places I could only dream of, from Lynn shooting the Beatles at Maple Leaf Gardens in 1964, to Doug being locked in a dressing room with Mick Jagger in London, Ont. in 1965, from developing film in airport toilets to meet their newspaper deadlines, to following the high and mighty. From popes and queens and politicians of every ilk, to sports stars and their fans and to everyday people, Lynn and Doug have created images of Canada and Canadians that have made history and will become a legacy for generations of Canadians.
– *John Major, director of photography, The Ottawa Citizen*

You thought you had seen, read, or heard it all. You haven't. Until now! Lynn and Doug are among the best photojournalists in the country and they've got decades of stories to share with you. Their eyes missed little – their lens missed nothing. And now they're telling you the stories behind the pictures.

I've had the privilege of working alongside both in the pivotal years of the '60s and '70s, and then watched with admiration as they continued to chronicle the history of this wonderful country. They have a passion for the art and an appreciation of the soul of the country. Enjoy their superb contribution to building a better Canada.
– *Max Keeping, CJOH/CTV News vice-president*

Since the 1960s Canadian photojournalism has been dominated by Balls, brothers Lynn and Doug in particular. They took many of the most memorable Canadian news photos of the past 40 years. With Lynn at *The Ottawa Citizen* and Doug at *The Canadian Press*, there was often a Ball photo on the front pages of the country's newspapers. These intrepid siblings would frequently return from assignments with pictures that would surprise and delight their editors. Their stories of how the photos were taken were sometimes even better. Many of these great news photos and the stories behind them are collected here for the first time. This is a great tribute to two remarkable photographers and their impact on photojournalism in Canada.
– *Russ Mills, Executive Dean, Faculty of Arts, Media and Design, Algonquin College, former editor and publisher of The Ottawa Citizen.*

Journalists love to describe their work as 'history on the run'. That is true but some times with each retelling of those stories the history gets a little better! Not so with the Ball brothers – their history is locked on film and never changes. Their pictures tell the story of a fascinating time in Canadian life.
– *Peter Mansbridge, CBC Television News*

Caught With His Pants Down

By Lynn Ball

How did I get my first job at *The Canadian Press*? I caught a man with his pants down!

I have two enduring passions: cars and photography. In 1963, I was an office boy at *The London Free Press* running copy and bringing coffee to the reporters and editors. One weekend in June, I got a freelance assignment to cover a race at Harewood Acres, Ont., for an American magazine, *Today's Motorsports*, in Gary, Ind.

I didn't know it but my career was about to move into high gear. As I watched the races, a race car spun out of control. The car was a modified Sadler MK V with its engine in the rear and its radiator in the front. As the Sadler lurched to a stop, steam began rising in clouds from the car's cockpit.

The driver jumped out running, pulling his pants down as he ran. A radiator hose had ruptured, spraying him with scalding water. He wasn't seriously hurt and it was an amusing sight for onlookers. I caught the stripdown on film with a Rolleiflex camera.

The London Free Press ran the series of four photos on Page One. Then *The Canadian Press* moved the pictures to its member papers across Canada. The *Associated Press* wire service based in New York moved it around the world.

My photos of the driver with his pants down won *The Canadian Press* Picture of the Month award and the Professional Photographers of Canada picture story of the year award.

Thanks to that award, and the recommendations of *London Free Press* managing editor Ivor Williams, I landed a job at *The Canadian Press* in Toronto, working in the darkroom.

Lynn's four pictures of a race-car driver bailing out from a hot seat won him two awards and his first job at The Canadian Press. /Lynn Ball

The Faces of Hate

By Lynn Ball

This article appeared in MEDIA, Fall/Winter 2003

When he was a young and hungry photographer, Lynn Ball travelled to America's Deep South to witness a scene he'll never forget.

In the fall of 1963, I was working as an office boy and darkroom replacement at *The London Free Press*. Managing editor Ivor Williams told me he had recommended me to *Canadian Press* in Toronto for a job in their darkroom. I had just won a *CP* picture of the month and wanted to move on and up to become a news photographer.

I got the job. It was a wonderful opportunity to learn the ins and outs. I was working in the darkroom when U.S. president John F. Kennedy was shot. I took wire pictures for 36 hours non-stop; I also watched Winston Churchill's funeral and many other world events through the wire negatives in the *CP* darkroom.

This fuelled my passion for photography and I began shooting any event that I could as a freelancer: The Beatles, NHL hockey including Stanley Cups with the Toronto Maple Leafs winning. Can you imagine that?

The civil rights movement in the southern United States was heating up and I followed the movement with great interest. When it was announced

Governor George Wallace in the Alabama Legislature. /Lynn Ball

that Martin Luther King Jr. was to lead a 50-mile march from Selma, Ala. to Montgomery, I had a feeling this was going to be an historic event.

I decided to take a few days off and drive south to take some photos that might help advance my career from a darkroom technician to a news photographer. Back then, Interstate 75 went only as far as Cincinnati; the rest of the way south was two lanes through the small towns of mountainous Tennessee and Kentucky with such memorable names as Rabbit Hash, Ky. I arrived from Toronto in steamy Montgomery 25 hours later. A visit to the police station secured a media card, and then I found the motel where *Associated Press* had set up shop. I met the photographers, who were hard as nails.

I followed a civil rights demonstration from a black neighbourhood to the State Legislature. The building was ringed with police.

Civil rights leaders Ralph Abernathy, Martin Luther King and Ralph Bunche. /Lynn Ball

White protestors against integration shocked young Lynn Ball when he visited Selma, Ala., in the spring of 1965. /Lynn Ball

Civil rights protestor Willie Ricks asks a state trooper to let him walk on the sidewalk. /Lynn Ball

They wouldn't let the demonstrators use the sidewalk, forcing them to walk on the road. The demonstrators pleaded with police to let them march on the sidewalk, but the police refused. It was illegal to walk on the road. You had to be on the sidewalk. So the police vans came and they all were arrested for marching on the road, and not on the sidewalk.

This march was led by two young men—one was white, the other black. The black man spoke to the police who were blocking the way onto the sidewalk. He said, "My name is Willie Ricks. I'm from Tennessee and I want to walk on the sidewalk. Governor Wallace says I can walk on the sidewalk. Please let me on the sidewalk."

The police would not let them on the sidewalks, hence the arrests.

Three years after this demonstration, Willie Ricks would become Brother Mukasa Ricks and ally himself with Stokely Carmichael. Ricks was the first member of the Student Non-Violent Coordinating Committee (SNCC) to use the call-and-response chant "What do we want? Black power!" This is the scene that I expected. This is what newspapers and television news showed.

Hearing of a white demonstration, I went to have a look. I was shocked. White people marched, carried racist placards and verbally abused any blacks who marched past them. I couldn't believe the language. Some of the women had fouler mouths than the men. I witnessed several white rallies and really had a hard time understanding what was going on. Housewives, their hair in curlers, carried signs with the words "WHO NEEDS NIGGERS?"

The time was near for the start of the march led by Martin Luther King Jr., so I drove over to Selma and got my press card from the infamous Jim Clark, sheriff of Selma. I was at the church bright and early where the long march to Montgomery was to begin. Speakers Ralph Abernathy, Ralph Bunche and Martin Luther King Jr. got the crowd in the mood and they were soon on the road.

It was an unforgettable sight to see the demonstrators march across the bridge over the Alabama River. The next day I headed north for Toronto as I had to get back to work. It was nice to get home.

Lynn Ball secured the promotion he longed for, becoming The Canadian Press's first news photographer, a position he was given after shooting the pictures of the demonstration in Selma.

Protestors line up for supper on the first night out from Selma on the 50-mile march to Montgomery. /Lynn Ball

The Beatles meet the press, Maple Leaf Gardens, 1964. /Lynn Ball

MAPLE LEAF GARDENS LIMITED
ATTRACTION PASS

11

Issued to ......*Lyn Ball*......
Representing ......*Canadian* ~~Ball~~ *Press*......
Good only ......*Sept 7*......

ADMIT AT ANY PASS GATE

A Bunch of Long-haired Loonies

By Lynn Ball

After a weekend at Sauble Beach on Lake Huron, I had to get back to Toronto to cover the Beatles' arrival on Sept. 7, 1964.

How could everyone be caught up by a bunch of long-haired loonies? I wondered.

The British Phenom met the press before performing at Maple Leaf Gardens. It was a circus. It took place on the stage and anyone who was anyone was there. Miss Canada, recording company executives, media types. Even the mayor of Kingston, who presented the Beatles with a gift from his city.

John, Paul, George and Ringo posed happily for endless pictures, gave interviews, met the celebrities, chatting with anyone who wanted to chat, and generally hammed it up, it seemed, for their own amusement.

"We would like you to meet 14-year-old Canadian TV star Michelle Finney," the MC announced.

Finney, host of the CBC kids' show *Razzle Dazzle*, looked much older than her years. The Beatles were paying only half attention, but when Ringo noticed Finney, he pushed himself through the crowd and, looking her up and down, announced in his thick Liverpool accent, "She's only fo'teen" to howls of laughter from onlookers.

I introduced myself and shook hands with each member of the band. It wasn't until many years later that I realized how special this was. We've all seen them come and go but the Beatles endure. In September 1964, these were normal guys having a good time.

(Within a year, their next visit to Toronto, Aug. 17, 1965, was very different. The press conference was very organized and there was no personal contact. Fame changed things.)

After the press conference, we waited for the concert to start. The opening acts were great including Jackie de Shannon, but it didn't

The Beatles with Michelle Finney, star of Razzle Dazzle. /Lynn Ball

matter, the hype was up for the Beatles. They came on stage to piercing screams and blinding flash bulbs that lit the Gardens for the entire performance.

Shrieking girls kept it up, easing off a little between songs, but as soon as the Fab Four started singing the screaming resumed. The noise was painful and my ears were ringing for a few days afterwards.

St. John Ambulance uniformed nurses carried out countless women who were in total uncontrollable hysterics. After the show it took awhile to find the young women who had passed out and were lying on the floor between the rows of seats.

Toronto Star photographer Reg Innell borrowed two bullets from a police officer and used them as earplugs.

During the performance, George Harrison came to the edge of the stage where I was standing. I aimed my camera and he leaned over towards me. I took the shot. I had Ilford FP3 film in my 35 mm Konica and used direct flash. The flash was powered with six D cell batteries. When the batteries were new, they took 22 seconds to recycle, but after just a few shots, recycle time went to more than 30 seconds. So, it was a one-shot effort. The film, 125 ASA, was fine grain and even though the pictures were shot on 35 mm film, they still make wonderful 16X20 inch prints.

(*The Ottawa Citizen* ran this photo of Harrison full page when he died on Dec. 1, 2001, aged 58, after a long fight against cancer.)

The concert ended and after watching the hysterical women being dragged out, I went back to *The Canadian Press* darkroom to process, print and transmit the pictures over the wirephoto network.

Then I returned to the Gardens for the Beatles' evening show. It was interesting watching the crowd funnel into the stadium, knowing what they were in for.

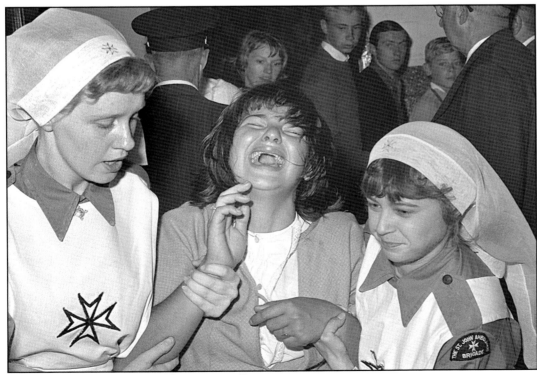

Nurses carry away a hysterical fan. /Lynn Ball

Ringo Starr, John Lennon, Paul McCartney and George Harrison meet the press on their second tour in 1965. /Lynn Ball

George Harrison leans towards the camera to accommodate the photographer. /Lynn Ball

Lessons from The Rolling Stones

By Doug Ball

The Rolling Stones taught me a great Boy Scout lesson in photography: Be Prepared.

Way back when I was at home in London, Ont., learning a little about photography from Dad, I had a part-time job in a department store photo shop.

One day in late April 1965, the Sayvette's manager asked me to go to the arena where the London junior hockey team played and take some pictures of a rock and roll group he had fronted to play at Treasure Island Gardens.

I was in my last year of high school and wondered who the group was. Well, "Ladies and gentlemen, The Rolling Stones!" I took the assignment.

My manager Pat Quinn wanted some photos to promote Stones' records at the store and hoped he'd make some money on ticket sales on the night, April 26.

I went to the Gardens a couple of hours early to get some shots of the band members before the concert. A girl I knew at G.A. Wheable High School in London was an absolute Rolling Stones nut. She was also the top student in the school. "How does that work?" I wondered. She'd taken the day off school so she could line up early to get into the mosh pit, a sought-after spot on the floor in front of the stage.

Before the show, I walked to the front from the backstage area and saw her squashed against the arena doors unable to move but still smil-

Keith Richards and Brian Jones, London, Ont., 1965. /Doug Ball

ing. I went into the dressing room and spent nearly an hour there talking mostly to drummer Charlie Watts. I took a few pictures of the Stones sitting around waiting and drinking. I took a shot of the group with a disc jockey from a local radio station. Then I asked Mick Jagger to lean over and look in the mirror, which he did, and I got a great photograph.

Twenty minutes into the concert all hell broke loose. After the Stones played a few songs the fence in front of the stage came down and that was it! The show was over. Fearing the crowd was getting out of control, the police pulled the plug on the lights and sound.

Not yet a news photographer, I lost out on an historic moment in rock and roll. I didn't take any photos of the action. Instead, I ran to get out of the way of stampeding fans. I call this one of my learning assignments.

The Rolling Stones in London, Ont., 1965. From left: Bill Wyman, Brian Jones, Keith Richards, local DJ Paul Ski, Mick Jagger, Charlie Watts. /Doug Ball

A mirror image of Mick Jagger. /Doug Ball

A rare occurrence: Leafs celebrate winning the Stanley Cup in 1964. In this picture are, from top, clockwise, Allan Stanley, Andy Bathgate, Eddie Shack, Tim Horton, Bob Pulford, Bob Baun, George Armstrong, Carl Brewer, Billy Harris, Larry Hillman, Jim Pappin, Ron Stewart, Johnny Bower and trainer Bob Haggart. Note the microphone dangling in front of the Stanley Cup. /Lynn Ball

MAPLE LEAF GARDENS LIMITED
NEWS PHOTOGRAPHERS PASS 22

Issued to Lynn Ball

Representing Canadian Press

Good only HOCKEY

ADMIT AT ANY PASS GATE (IMPORTANT OVER)

When Shack Shook the Gardens

By Lynn Ball

A perk that went with my job as a darkroom technician for *The Canadian Press* was a freelance gig shooting Toronto Maple Leafs' home games.

I was competing with photographers from the city's big dailies, *The Toronto Star*, *Toronto Telegram* and *The Globe and Mail,* to supply photos to the *CP* picture service. They got me a pass to Maple Leaf Gardens and I was paid $5 for every picture used on the wire.

The Leafs played home games most Wednesdays and Saturdays. I don't think I missed a game. I photographed the Leafs winning the Stanley Cup in 1964 and the picture of the hockey players around the trophy is still one of my favourites.

Hockey in that time in the 1960s, before expansion, was wonderful. Watching Bobby Hull, Gordie Howe, Frank Mahovlich, Jean Beliveau, Johnny Bower and other greats play the game will be with me always.

Nothing can match the energy of Eddie Shack bursting onto the ice when coach Punch Imlach would turn him loose, after rousing pleas from the crowd chanting, "WE WANT SHACK, WE WANT SHACK!" The Gardens shook to its foundation.

Robert and Ethel Kennedy enjoyed a hockey game after being guests at a Canadian Press dinner. /Doug Ball, Canadian Press

Broadcaster Ward Cornell interviews Leafs captain George Armstrong with Stanley Cup. /Lynn Ball

Terry Sawchuk and Johnny Bower, an awesome duo in the Leafs' nets in the 1960s. /Lynn Ball

Canadiens coach Toe Blake embraces Montreal centre Henri Richard after knocking the Leafs out of the playoffs in 1965. /Lynn Ball

Leafs coach Punch Imlach (centre) chats with his goalies, Johnny Bower (left) and Terry Sawchuk at Peterborough training camp. /Lynn Ball

Canadiens' Henri Richard and Leafs' Eddie Shack mix it up along the boards. /Lynn Ball

STANLEY CUP PLAYOFFS
1965
PRESS CARD

PHOTO

083 9 Lynn Ball
Canadian Press

*Montreal Canadiens Henri Richard, Jean Beliveau and John Ferguson
celebrate the elimination of the Leafs from the NHL playoffs at Maple
Leaf Gardens in April 1965. /Lynn Ball*

Despite his best acrobatic manoeuvres, Leafs goalie Johnny Bower sometimes missed, as in this photo. /Lynn Ball

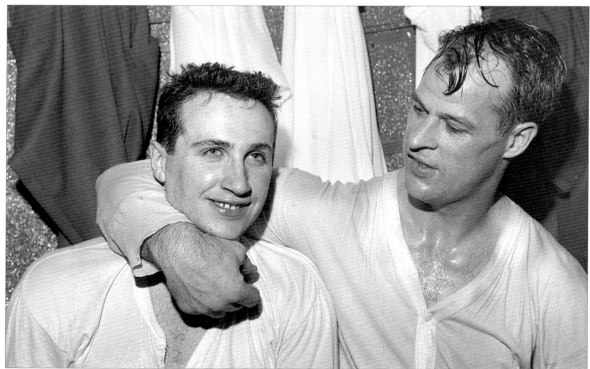

Gordie Howe wraps a massive arm around fellow Red Wing Ed Joyal. /Lynn Ball

Gordie Howe, a.k.a. Mr. Elbows, stamps his trademark on the neck of Quebec Nordique Curt Brackenbury. /Doug Ball, Canadian Press

Richard Burton embraces actress Eileen Hurlie. /Lynn Ball

I Know Liz and Dick, but Who's Sir John?

By Lynn Ball

Things were wild in Hogtown as theatre history was being made. British actor Richard Burton was starring in Sir John Gielgud's production of Hamlet at the O'Keefe Centre running from Feb. 26 to March 21, 1964.

Elizabeth Taylor was in Toronto with him and rumours were rampant that they were going to get married.

Assigned to cover the play's opening night and take pictures of VIPs, I arrived at the centre to hear the crowd buzzing about Monk Marr's arrival. Who was Monk Marr? Turns out Ryerson Polytechnical Institute students, mingling with the crowd, were getting the stargazers hyped and excited about a non-existent celebrity. Monk Marr arrived in a Cadillac limousine with a mock police escort. Emerging to cheers from the crowd, Marr went on inside to enjoy Shakespeare. The college stunt, catching us off guard, created a lot of fun.

Now, I had to try for a shot of Burton's girlfriend. Several photographers staked out the back door of the O'Keefe Centre as snow fell. It was hard to keep my Rolleiflex and flash free of the wet flakes.

A Cadillac pulled up and out stepped the beautiful Elizabeth Taylor, decked in furs and diamonds and clutching a small purse. Flanked by escorts, the world-famous movie star walked through the falling snow and in through the stage door.

I had to get the film back to *The Canadian Press* darkroom as we had a flood of requests from *Associated Press* in New York and many newspapers. *The Ottawa Citizen* wanted four or five prints air expressed overnight. *The Detroit Free Press* had a special request as well.

Then I had to rush back to the O'Keefe Centre for more pictures after the performance. I made it into the Green Room before the actors entered. It was all a bit overwhelming, as I had never shot anything like this before. I got a shot of Richard Burton, cigarette in hand, holding Eileen Hurlie who played Gertrude. I took pictures of Hume Cronyn, a hit as Polonius, and the other players.

I got a shot of this fellow who looked important but I didn't know who he was.

"Can I get your name, sir?"

"Yes, it's Sir John Gielgud," he said in a withering tone indicating I should have known this.

What a night. Richard Burton, Elizabeth Taylor, Monk Marr and Sir John Gielgud.

The pictures of Taylor arriving and Burton and Hurlie together got great play the next day in newspapers across the continent. I was still a

Sir John Gielgud and Eileen Hurlie. /Lynn Ball

darkroom technician but I knew that if I worked hard I'd make it as a news photographer.

The Liz and Dick watch continued and they did, indeed, slip off on a quick trip to Montreal and were married.

They were divorced in 1974, remarried in 1975 and divorced again in 1976.

Movie star Elizabeth Taylor is escorted through a Toronto snowfall. /Lynn Ball

You Can't Top This!

By Lynn Ball

A Toronto swimwear manufacturer had a line of topless and transparent women's bathing suits to be presented at a show by the National Garment Salesmen's Association. It was June 1964, and one of my first photo assignments for *The Canadian Press* was to take photos of these new bathing suits. At the manufacturer's office, a hired model came out wearing one of the topless swimsuits. The manufacturer refused to let me take pictures as she "didn't show off the swimsuits to their best." In other words, she had very small breasts. He took his secretary aside and then said to me that we had our model but asked me to be discreet in showing her face. So, wearing sunglasses or averting her face, the more amply endowed secretary posed in the swimsuits. Some things never change. *CP* editors ran the pictures on the wire but painted out the bare nipples and slugged it "BORDERLINE."

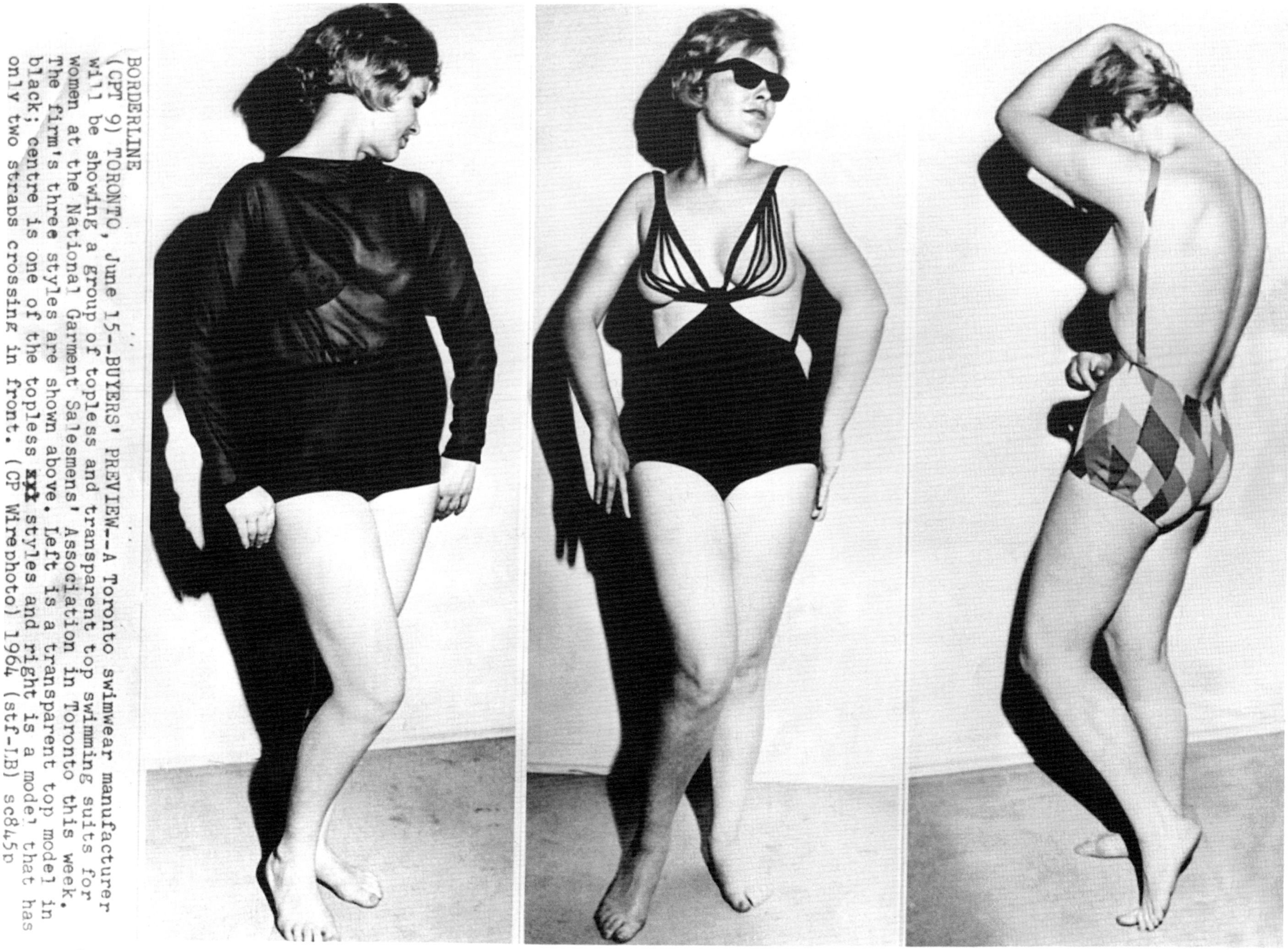

BORDERLINE
(CPT 9) TORONTO, June 15--BUYERS' PREVIEW--A Toronto swimwear manufacturer will be showing a group of topless and transparent top swimming suits for women at the National Garment Salesmens' Association in Toronto this week. The firm's three styles are shown above. Left is a transparent top model in black; centre is one of the topless xxi styles and right is a model that has only two straps crossing in front. (CP Wirephoto) 1964 (stf-LB) sc845p

Lynn Ball

Northern Dancer Won but Choppum Please Paid Off

By Lynn Ball

As a yearling, Northern Dancer couldn't sell for $25,000 so owner E.P. Taylor kept him. It proved a wise decision. Two years later the chunky bay became Canada's horse, winning the 1964 Kentucky Derby over Hill Rise, America's favourite, by a neck and setting a Derby record of two minutes flat.

Then it was on to the Preakness in Baltimore, Md. At Pimlico Racetrack, Northern Dancer won again, this time by two-and-a-quarter lengths over The Scoundrel. Hill Rise was third.

The Belmont, the final event of The Triple Crown at Aqueduct Racetrack, Jamaica, N.Y., was the beginning of the end of the little horse's racing days. Northern Dancer injured a tendon in his left front leg and finished third.

The Queen's Plate, June 20, 1964, at Toronto's Woodbine Racetrack was Northern Dancer's last race. He won by seven-and-a-half lengths on three legs. The tendon in his left foreleg was severely strained.

It was like a dream to be at these events. The crowd was wild with anticipation and Northern Dancer did not disappoint. He was running dead last then like a rocket took off passing all of the other horses with ease.

I got shots of the finish with my 35 mm and headed for the winner's circle where I was lucky enough to get a shot with my Rolleiflex of North-ern Dancer, E.P. Taylor, jockey Bill Hartack, still in the saddle, and groom Bill Brevard. The two-and-a-quarter inch square negatives, sharp as a tack and fine grain, make great enlargements even now. Lit beautifully by the sun, it's a full side view of Northern Dancer with his injured foreleg slightly lifted.

I didn't bet on Northern Dancer. He was a 1-7 favourite and there wasn't much of a payoff. Many bettors kept the winning Northern Dancer ticket as a souvenir. But I did bet $2 on a horse in an earlier race, I think it was called Choppum Please. It won and paid me $17, a tidy little sum because I was getting only $5 per picture moved on the wire from *The Canadian Press*.

In December 1964 Canada's leading sports writers and editors named Northern Dancer Canada's athlete of the year – the first time for a horse and never since.

After his winning season, Northern Dancer retired and became the greatest stud horse in history. By the time of his death on Nov. 16, 1990, he had fathered 467 winners, including more than 150 stake race winners. In total, he sired 635 registered foals. It's estimated that his bloodlines extend to more than half of all thoroughbred horses.

Northern Dancer with owner E.P. Taylor, groom Bill Brevard and jockey Bill Hartack in the winner's circle, 1964 Queen's Plate. /Lynn Ball

A young boy blocks the skirl of the bagpipes from his ears at the opening of the Confederation Centre of the Arts in Charlottetown, 1964. /Lynn Ball

God Saves the Queen

By Lynn Ball

In September 1964, while I was toiling as a darkroom technician for *The Canadian Press* in Toronto, I was covering any and all events whenever possible in the hopes someone would notice my hard work. Finally it paid off. I got my first big assignment – Queen Elizabeth II and Prince Philip's visit to Eastern Canada.

A few days before the royal couple was to arrive in Prince Edward Island, my boss Tom Williams and I flew to Moncton, N.B., on a TCA Viscount (my first trip on a large aircraft) and then on to Charlottetown, P.E.I., on a small plane that made a very rough landing.

We booked into our room at the Queen's Hotel, an old wooden building that not surprisingly burned to the ground a short time later. That night we shared the cramped quarters with radio newsman J.J. Richards, who slept on the floor, as his reservation hadn't worked out.

We moved to another hotel the next day and met up with the crew from *Associated Press* out of Boston, darkroom technician Jack Bradley and photographer Walter Green as well as photographers Charlie Kelly from the southern U.S. and my hero, Preston Stroup, a Texan based in Michigan. I had asked what he drove, and in his Texas drawl he said that he drove both a Corvette and a Cadillac. Who wouldn't have a successful news photographer with a Corvette and a Cadillac as a hero?

We set up a darkroom in Summerside in a men's washroom in order to transmit pictures of the Queen's arrival. The water running down a urinal when flushed was ideal for washing negatives. Another darkroom was set up in Charlottetown.

The royals flew into Summerside but the events were staged in the provincial capital, Charlottetown. They were staying on the royal yacht Britannia during the visit.

One night, I was at the Britannia to photograph the Queen and Prince Philip boarding the ship following the day's events. As the couple approached a small stage with the yacht's gangplank resting on top of it, they stopped briefly to acknowledge the crowd. As they turned again towards the gangplank to board, the stage suddenly lurched back and flipped over. In a truly God-save-the-Queen moment, they weren't on it.

The ship, rising with the tide, had pulled the gangplank to the edge of the stage causing the platform to flip. Organizers hadn't made allowances for nature.

The next day, a band was playing on the street at the opening of the new Confederation Centre of the Arts, a tribute to our founding fathers. I spotted a father and son, the boy standing with his hands over his ears to block out the skirl of the bagpipes. *AP* moved my photo of the unhappy boy on the world network and it got worldwide play.

In Quebec, the numbers turned out for the Queen's visit as they did in P.E.I., but many people didn't want her there and they made sure we knew it. There were numerous demonstrations and some turned violent.

The Royal 22nd Regiment was celebrating its 50th anniversary and the Queen debarked the royal yacht to inspect the Honour Guard, lined up and ready in the dockside arrival shed at Anse-au-Foulon.

Just before the Queen entered, a soldier fainted and fell to the ground. He was dragged quickly away as she began her inspection. The picture of the prostrate guard with his fellow soldiers gazing ahead as if nothing had happened won me a major award for news photography.

That evening I was assigned to cover an anti-monarchist rally at Laval University. A protester was wearing a pair of underwear on the outside of his pants with a sign painted across the back saying "GOD SHIT THE QUEEN."

I was wearing a beret I'd picked up in a spree with the other photogs covering the Queen's visit in Quebec City. In P.E.I., we'd all purchased tams in the provincial tartan and wore them. In a sign of the times, the speaker at the rally stopped in mid-flow and came over to me. He said something in French to the amusement of the demonstrators who were laughing and pointing at me.

When I said I didn't speak French, someone translated the speaker's remarks: "Only women wear hats inside."

I just smiled, kept my hat on and the anti-Queen protest carried on. It was a bit rough in there for awhile but we all made out okay.

Stroup found a giant cigarette lighter that took several containers of lighter fluid to fill it up. He thought it was strange that he had to come to Quebec City to find a Texas-sized lighter.

What a mess our darkroom was in the Chateau Frontenac, with developers and fixer fluids slopped all over the place in a rush to get the pictures out as quickly as possible. But we did it, mess or no. My time spent with the seasoned *AP* photographers under deadline pressure taught me a lot.

Queen Elizabeth in Prince Edward Island, 1964. Lynn Ball, Canadian Press

A guardsman passed out just before the Queen was to pass by. /Lynn Ball, Canadian Press

Lynn Ball

lv Tor TCA Flt 420 1 p.m.
    connects at Mctn for flite to Chtwn   WITH TW

lv Chtwn for Que via charter   WITH TW

Lv Que for Tor 525p Oct. 11 TCA Flt 451
    connects at Mtl for flite to Tor

    (This is a no cancel ticket—it will be held to
    flight time—but if at all possible LB shud call
    TCA Que and re-confirm six hours prior to departure)

The Queen inspecting the Royal 22nd Regiment at Quebec City. /Lynn Ball, Canadian Press

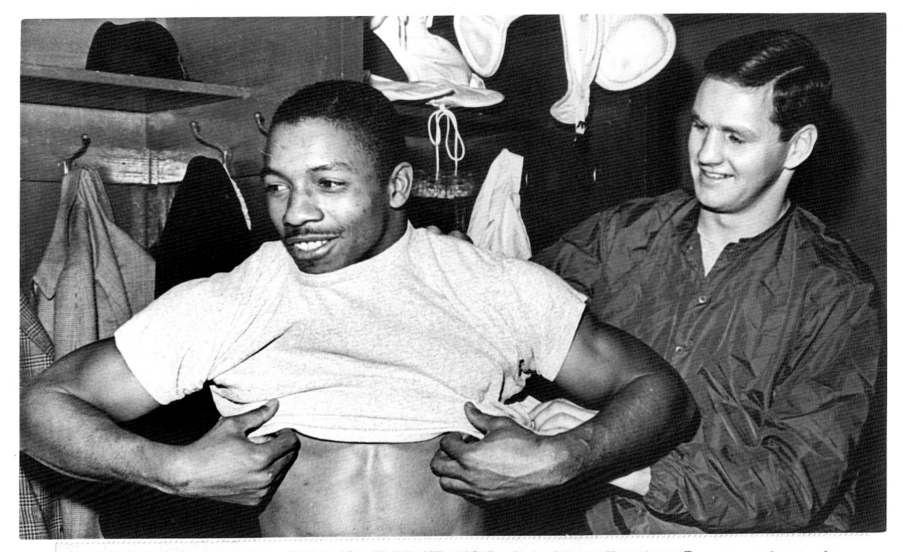

(CPT 23) TORONTO, Nov. 24--LIONS ARE READY AND EAGER--B.C. Lions flew into Toronto today to keep their Saturday date with Hamilton Tiger Cats in the Grey Cup game. Lions wasted no time sitting around but headed for Varsity Stadium for a workout a few minutes after they arrived at their hotel. Here Willie Fleming gets a helping tug from Jim Carphin as the team got into practice gear in the stadium dressing room. (CP Wirephoto) 1964 (stf-LB) eds853p

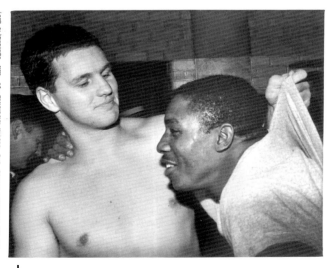

Jim Carphin and Willie Fleming
celebrate the Lions' Grey Cup
victory over the
Hamilton Tiger Cats, 1964.
Lynn Ball, Canadian Press

Lynn
Many thanks
for the photos. That
was a fine shot of the
T.D.. You must have expected
it more than I did. See
you in Toronto next year.
J.

A Magical 1964 Grey Cup

By Lynn Ball

In the fall of 1963, I was working in the darkroom taking the wire transmissions for *The Canadian Press* in Toronto of the Grey Cup game in Vancouver. I wished I were out there shooting football not stuck in the stinking darkroom.

A year later, my wish came true. The defending champion Hamilton Tiger Cats would be playing the B.C. Lions at Toronto's CNE Stadium, a rematch of the 1963 Grey Cup. This was a big deal for me and at that time Grey Cup football was a big deal for Canada.

It was an entire week of practices, receptions, beauty contests, banquets and a football game. I was assigned to cover the B.C. Lions practices.

The Lions flew into Toronto on Tuesday Nov. 24, checked into their hotel and wasted no time getting to Varsity Stadium to practice. I got into the Lions' dressing room while they were getting ready.

Willie Fleming was the Lions star running back and I thought I should try for a picture of him suiting up for practice. I went over and talked to Fleming and he agreed to have a picture taken with offensive end Jim Carphin helping him dress by pulling down his sweater.

TRANSMITTED IN RESPONSE TO A REQUEST
(CPT 9-Dec. 29) GREY CUP PASS--This photo of Joe Kapp of B.C. Lions throwing pass while being tackled byPete Neumann of Hamilton during this year's Grey Cup, is transmitted in response to a request. (CP Wirephoto) 1964 (fls-Stf) rxvllp

I took many more pictures at practice that day and several moved on the *CP* wire nationally including the shot of Fleming and Carphin.

The next day when I arrived at practice I was walking along the sidelines when I saw Fleming doing an interview with CTV's Johnny Esau. As I passed him, Willie motioned for me to wait for him.

When the interview was over, Willie invited me into the dressing room. Other players started calling out, "Trainer, get me some tapes. Trainer, fix my pads."

Then Carphin came over and asked, "Why did you call me trainer in that photo you took yesterday?"

The Globe and Mail had run the photo and rewritten the caption referring to Carphin in error as "trainer" so his teammates were joking around with it.

Fortunately it was all in fun and I was accepted as almost one of the team from then on. I covered the Miss Grey Cup beauty contest and the awards banquet. But the game itself was the big deal.

Hamilton had defeated Vancouver 21-10 in 1963, so the Lions had made a 1964 win in the east a priority. In the second quarter while leading 7-0, the Lions were going to attempt a field goal from the Tiger Cats' 19-yard line.

Lions' Pete Ohler fumbled the snap so he couldn't set the ball on the ground for the field goal. Ohler retrieved the ball and threw an end zone pass to Carphin in a broken play that ended with a touchdown. Carphin was a second string end sent on the field by Lions coach Dave Skrien as an emergency receiver in the event of a bad snap.

Fleming had been a thorn in the paw of the Tiger Cats all afternoon. He scampered around the end for a 46-yard touchdown, ending the day with 67 yards on six rushes and catching two passes for 36 yards.

Led by quarterback Joe Kapp, soon to be a star in the National Football League, the B.C. Lions won the Grey Cup 34-24 over the Hamilton Tiger Cats.

It was wild in the Lions' dressing room after the game and magic for me. A lot of champagne went down as all of the players took turns drinking from the Cup.

I got Willie Fleming and Jim Carphin together for another picture. Carphin wrote me asking for prints of the nice picture I took of his touchdown. I sent him a package and he sent me back a letter and a Christmas card. Of all the Grey Cups I covered in later years, none would compare with this one.

Tables Turned On Miss Grey Cup

By Lynn Ball

Over the years I developed a quick shutter finger for I never knew when a good photo would come along.

In the mid-1960s, beauty pageants were hot news and the crowning of Miss Grey Cup was second only to the football game itself. The lovely contestants, representing each football team in the Canadian Football League, were judged with great fanfare and the winner was announced at the Miss Grey Cup Pageant. The pageant was part of the annual autumn carnival known as Grey Cup Week, which culminated in Canada's most-watched football game.

This time, things took a different turn on Friday, Nov. 27, 1964 as photographers were shooting Miss Grey Cup and the two runners-up. Al Lieshman of *The Montreal Star* had the bright idea of posing the three young beauty queens on the edge of a table that was loaded with food for the reception after the pageant.

The table collapsed just as the three women settled themselves, sending plates and food crashing to the floor. Carrol Taylor, Miss Calgary Stampeder, Susan Browne, Miss Grey Cup and Holly Evans, Miss Winnipeg Blue Bomber, somehow kept their balance, if not their dignity.

My picture caught the moment. Everyone else missed it, including Lieshman, who is standing on the right.
Lynn Ball, Canadian Press

Hosed at Work

On my way to work at *The Canadian Press* in Toronto where I was a darkroom technician, I saw firemen fighting a warehouse fire. A fireman at the top of a ladder had lost pressure in his hose and was dousing his mate on a ladder below him. The picture won *CP* picture of the month for May 1965. It was the first time a *CP* staffer had won the award since it had been instituted in 1949. /*Lynn Ball*

Dief was at home everywhere, whether speaking in the Commons or meeting a garbage man. /Lynn Ball, Canadian Press

The Man from Prince Albert

By Lynn Ball

John Diefenbaker was at home with anyone, anywhere. There wasn't a voter he didn't care to greet.

The 1965 federal election was one of my first major assignments as Ottawa-based national staff photographer for *The Canadian Press*. I joined Progressive Conservative leader John Diefenbaker's campaign in Pembroke, Ont. and we worked our way through the Ottawa Valley to the capital.

We stopped wherever people were spotted so Dief could shake hands with them and at scheduled stops in the towns of Cobden and Renfrew. We also stopped at the place where a small cairn announced that explorer Samuel de Champlain's astrolabe had been found there in 1867.

Standing by the monument, the Progressive Conservative leader declared that if elected prime minister he would bring the historic artifact, willed to The New York Historical Society by its owner in 1942, back to Canada. The astrolabe, an essential tool of exploration and navigation used to determine the altitude of stars and planets, was lost on Champlain's trek up the Ottawa River in 1613.

We drove on to Renfrew to do some mainstreeting. Dief thrived on this. He walked through the town's commercial centre shaking hands with everyone he met. He went into the men's clothing store and bought a new tie. Then Renfrew's garbage truck pulled up. The unshaven and scruffy looking garbage man got out of the cab and the Tory leader walked into the street to meet him and shake his hand.

It was my best shot of the day and *The Globe and Mail* ran it very large on Page One.

It was fun on the campaign with Dief. With security the way it is today, his populist style is a thing of the past.

After all my years of following politicians, "the man from Prince Albert" is still my favourite.

John George Diefenbaker, Canada's 13th prime minister (1957-1963), was an eloquent spokesman for the "non-establishment". From winning the largest majority in Canadian history in 1958, he stumbled to a minority government in 1962 and total defeat in 1963.

Champlain's astrolabe, found after 254 years near Cobden, Ont. in 1867 by a 14-year-old farm boy, Edward Lee, is on view at the Museum of Civilization. The museum acquired the astrolabe from The New York Historical Society in June 1989.

Lynn Ball talking with John Diefenbaker, his favourite politician, in 1967.

Oh, for goodness sakes! Prime Minister Lester Pearson watches the Canadian flag unfurl upside down in his home riding of Algoma. Lynn Ball, Canadian Press

Upside Down in Elliot Lake

By Lynn Ball

One of Lester Pearson's greatest accomplishments was giving Canada its own flag. Still, it had been a divisive national issue. Little wonder he was upset by my picture of it flying upside down, an international signal of distress.

It happened in late June 1966. Prime Minister Pearson, members of his staff and media travelled to Elliot Lake, a uranium-mining town in the prime minister's riding, Algoma East. The Viscount aircraft landed in Sudbury where Pearson met Ontario Premier John Robarts and the two leaders were then driven by limousine to Elliot Lake.

The rest of us boarded a Department of Lands and Forests* Otter aircraft with pontoons and seating for 11 passengers. It was a far cry from today when a large jet is required for all of the media and the prime minister's entourage when flying across the country and abroad.

Pearson went to a picnic at Flack Lake, St. Jean Baptiste Day celebrations, and a pub in the Nordic Hotel where he had a glass of ginger ale and sang with the locals in the bar. Outside, participants in the small St. Jean Baptiste Day parade passed by the prime minister as he stood on a makeshift stage. Afterwards, he was invited to see the raising of the country's new red maple leaf flag inaugurated on Feb. 15, 1965. A boy scout pulled on the rope. To everyone's embarrassment the flag unfurled upside down.

The media and the PM's entourage were flying on the Otter to Gore Bay on Manitoulin Island where the Viscount would take all of us to Toronto. Pearson was planning to fly to Gore Bay in a new Lands and Forests plane, a Turbo Beaver.

The PM's press secretary asked if I wanted to fly with Pearson as he would be taking the controls and it might make a good photo. The Otter took off first but when the Beaver was loaded there wasn't a seat for me.

They took off and I was left behind, stranded in Elliot Lake. Not only no photo of Pearson, no ride either.

On the other side of the wharf an older Lands and Forests Beaver was being loaded with boxes and other cargo. The pilot was headed for Gore Bay in a few minutes so if I could fit in, he'd give me a lift. I slid in on top of the gear and we landed on the water in Gore Bay. A guy in a pick-up truck gave me a wild ride to the airport where the Viscount was in the final stages of boarding.

On the way to Toronto, Pearson sought me out. Sitting alongside, he explained that the upside down flag was a mistake and they were all good people in Elliot Lake and wouldn't have done it on purpose.

A *Canadian Press* runner picked up my film on arrival in Toronto and my job was done.

Next morning Page One of *The Globe and Mail* displayed my picture of Pearson and the upside down flag. Pearson wasn't pleased. On the plane back to Ottawa, he chewed me out. In my defence, I said a *CP* photo-editor in Toronto had selected and moved the picture on the network. I wasn't even there.

To be honest, I would have used the same picture.

During this visit, there was one character I had trouble figuring out.

Pearson and Robarts had been greeted on their arrival by a man named Lionel. After lunch he got up and thanked Pearson for visiting Elliot Lake. As the two leaders were leaving, he hopped into the limousine with them.

That night, CBC newsman Tom Earle and camera man Bert Plimer had a small gathering of media and friends in their hotel room. Lionel showed up and made himself at home, especially with the liquor.

It was late. When Plimer and Earle suggested it was bedtime Lionel, the only remaining visitor, left but came back a few minutes later with a folding cot. He took a blanket and a pillow from the CBC representatives and they all went to bed.

In the morning he borrowed one of their razors, put on some gin as aftershave and left.

Since Lionel was in my pictures with Pearson and Robarts, I inquired as to who he was. Turned out he was the town character and had no official status. That just shows you how easygoing Pearson was. Today, Lionel would be arrested for trying to get into the PM's limo.

* *Ministry of Natural Resources today.*

Ontario Premier John Robarts meets Lester Pearson at Sudbury. Lynn Ball, Canadian Press

There's no seat for photographer Lynn Ball who was left stranded at the dock. /Lynn Ball, Canadian Press

Lester Pearson, who loved baseball, takes a mighty swing at the ball. /Lynn Ball, Canadian Press

Prime Minister Pearson joins a St. Jean Baptiste Day celebration in Elliot Lake. /Lynn Ball, Canadian Press

Pig in a Blanket

By Lynn Ball

For most of us, "pig in a blanket" means a sausage wrapped in pastry, a down-home hors d'oeuvre. But at the Chicoutimi farmers' market, in -40F weather, I found the real thing. Here was a swaddled pig – and a farmer protecting his investment from the cold. It was a heartwarming sort of picture that makes people smile.

I was in Chicoutimi, Que., in 1966 to cover the winter carnival for *The Canadian Press*. The town was celebrating the centennial of its post office and Postmaster General Jean-Pierre Côté was the carnival's guest of honour.

We flew from Ottawa to Bagotville, then caught the train for Chicoutimi. Our coach had plain wooden benches and a pot-bellied stove for heat. On our arrival, Côté, who had travelled first class, was presented at the train station with a beaver hat and a buffalo robe to keep him warm during the horse and buggy ride to the historic post office. CBC cameraman Rudy Wolf and I followed the procession in an open bus. We huddled in great discomfort on the floor of the bus, shivering in misery. Our warm coats were in luggage that had gone on ahead to the hotel.

Later, I set off to find a camp I'd heard about that was a recreation of a typical Indian village in pre-Confederation days. As I rounded a spruce tree, I came face to face with a large timber wolf, its fangs bared in a viscious snarl. After a few seconds of terror, I realized the wolf was dead. It was frozen solid and posed in front of an old-style deadfall trap.

Côté's staff requested the negatives of his trip for the post office magazine. They later told me they lost the film.

Côté was subsequently named to the Senate and then served as lieutenant-governor of Quebec from 1978 to 1984. All I have left of this assignment is one print of the picture I snapped of the pig in a blanket.

Lynn Ball, Canadian Press

Racing the Police and Steven Truscott

By Lynn Ball

In 1959, at 14, Steven Truscott became the youngest person to be sentenced to hang in Canada. He had been convicted of the rape and murder of schoolmate Lynne Harper, 12.

His sentence was eventually commuted to life. And in 1966, a book by Isabel LeBourdais, *The Trial of Steven Truscott*, sparked a huge public outcry. The federal government referred the controversial case to the Supreme Court of Canada. The two-week hearing started Oct. 5, 1966.

For the Truscott family, hope was high for Steven's release. They lived in Richmond, Ont., just outside Ottawa.

I was assigned to go out to their house and get a family picture. Trying to come up with an eye-catching picture of the family of four, I asked them

The Truscott family keeps a chair waiting for Steven. /Lynn Ball, Canadian Press

to stand around an empty chair to symbolize a place for Steven to sit when he came home.

The picture of the Truscotts grouped around an empty chair moved on *The Canadian Press* wirephoto network to all the major papers across the country.

The next day *The Toronto Telegram* ran the picture huge on Page One. The Steven Truscott story was theirs as writer LeBourdais, whose book had fueled the referral to the Supreme Court, worked for *The Telegram*.

Tely photographer Peter Geddes, in Ottawa doing pictures for the story, had spent a lot of time with the Truscotts. He wasn't pleased with me for beating him onto his paper's front page and the *Tely's* editors were not pleased with him, he said.

Steven Truscott arrived at court every day for the two-week hearing in a police car that drove right into the underground parking garage so it was impossible to get a picture of him.

CP had a lot of requests from its member newspapers for a picture of Truscott and *CP* photo editor Stan Mulcahy was after recent hire Chuck Mitchell and me everyday to get one as the case, the first time in its history that the Supreme Court heard live testimony, was the biggest story of the day.

We came up with a plan. I drove a Honda S600 sports coupe with a hatchback. I took the hatch off and we parked the Honda between two larger cars near the exit of the Supreme Court's underground parking lot.

Chuck got into the back with his cameras and I was at the wheel. We had to wait until the police car driving Truscott back to the Ottawa jail left the parking garage. We took off behind it.

When we turned onto Wellington Street, I pulled up beside the police car and Chuck, a giant at 6' 7", rose up from the hatch. He was less than a metre away from Truscott and shooting pictures like mad through the window of the police car.

It turned into a race. We stayed with the police car even through red lights. We followed them until they disappeared into the underground parking garage at the police station.

We pulled over and Chuck was getting into the front seat when the police officers that had been with Truscott came out of the station. We thought we were going to be arrested but they were happy to have a little excitement. They thought it was a good plan to try for a picture and were not upset at all.

Poor Stan, our boss, thought we were all going to end up in jail.

The picture wasn't great but at least we tried.

Steven Truscott's quest to clear his name has gone on for many years. On May 4, 1967, the Supreme Court of Canada voted 8-1 to uphold his conviction. He was paroled in 1969 after serving 10 years in prison. In 2000, Truscott went public again and a third book proclaiming his innocence was published. The case is now before the Ontario Court of Appeal.

The Open Fly Rule

By Lynn Ball

Parliament was sitting late into the night to get unanimous consent to end a 1966 dock strike in British Columbia. The other news photographers had gone for coffee when Labour Minister John Nicholson emerged from the House. I didn't want the other photogs to get a shot so I asked him for a picture in his office. He agreed and at my suggestion he posed, stretching to show how tired he was. That motion pulled up his suit exposing his open fly. I didn't want to spoil the picture so I shot a frame or two without mentioning the open fly, thanked him and left. With the help of some paint it was covered up for *Canadian Press* subscribers and the photo got good play. The original photo spent some time on the *CP* bulletin board. The Honourable John Robert (Jack) Nicholson P.C., O.B.E., Q.C., LL.D., LL.B., went on to become Lieutenant-Governor of British Columbia from 1968 to 1973.

Lynn Ball, Canadian Press

Canada's Pied Piper Led the Nation

By Lynn Ball

Canada! It was 1967 and Bobby Gimby's magical horn was trumpeting a bilingual vision for one and all. Every time you turned on the TV or radio during Canada's Centennial year you got to see and hear "Caaa-Naa-Da" like it or not. I finally saw him live and in action at the 1967 Grey Cup game at Lansdowne Park in Ottawa. "The Pied Piper of Canada" was leading a large group of children around the football field who were singing the Centennial Anthem. I ran in front of the parade with my IIIf Leica camera equipped with a 25mm Canon lens held over my head and got a couple of frames, a little bit of Canadian history.

Lynn Ball

Riding to School on a Wave

By Lynn Ball

With a near-record snowfall in the winter of 1972, the potential for a spring flood was high in the Ottawa Valley. The Rideau River did not let us down.

At the peak of the flood, *The Ottawa Citizen* sent me up in an airplane to look for a good picture. Flying above the Rideau, between the Ottawa Valley towns of Manotick and Kemptville, I could see that River Road was under water. Then I noticed a school bus approaching the flooded section of the road. I had the pilot circle above the bus and got several good shots with the sun backlighting the vehicle.

The school bus looked like a motor boat slicing through the water with the wake behind and the highway stretching ahead, the white line showing through the flood water.

There were no cell phones in those days. I asked the pilot to radio the tower at Uplands Airport and had the tower call *Citizen* managing editor Nelson Skuce to hold a spot on Page One.

We headed back to the airport and I hopped in the car and sped back to the paper, making deadline. The flood shot moved on *The Canadian Press* wire network and then won *The Canadian Press* Picture of the Month award.

In today's litigious society, school bus service seems to be cancelled at the slightest hint of environmental inconvenience. Imagine riding to school on a wave!

Lynn Ball, Ottawa Citizen

Lynn Ball, Ottawa Citizen

Summer's Bliss

By Lynn Ball

One summer's day as I left *The Ottawa Citizen* building to cross the Sparks Street Mall to the bank, I spotted a kid eating an ice cream cone. Was he enjoying it! Oblivious to everything except the ice cream, he was losing it to the hot sun. Melted ice cream covered his shirt; it was even dripping from his elbows. A large crowd watched in silence. Then the bottom fell out of the cone and a large lump of ice cream hit the ground. The kid started crying. His older brother, eyeing him from a distance in a store doorway, went into the store and came out with their mother. She consoled her son and cleaned him up with Kleenex. *The Citizen* ran several pictures showing the entire story. Readers got a taste of summer along with the boy and the crowd on the mall that hot, sunny day in the early '70s.

Metro Lady Cost Me Beer Money

By Doug Ball

In the 1970s, when I was a starving photographer for *The Canadian Press* news co-operative living off Montreal Forum hotdogs and Montreal Expos roast beef dinners at Jarry Park, it was always good to make a few extra dollars on an assignment.

I don't mean to say that we took bribes. Only, some days we ended up with more money in our pockets than we started with.

For example, one day I was at the headquarters of the National Hockey League at the Sun Life Building in Montreal's Dominion Square for the annual players' draft. League president Clarence Campbell ran the draft by conference call. It's not like today with everyone in one of the league's arenas under scrutiny by television cameras.

My assignment was to get some photos of Campbell starting the draft and then get some stuff of the Montreal Canadiens doing the pick from their Forum office. I figured they would have a lunch set up for the media.

Campbell was always a very boring subject to photograph. NHL officials sat at a table behind a grey speakerphone. No posters. No NHL signs. Nothing! I took a few shots and headed to the subway. My assignments were on the same Metro line.

If I took the Metro and then submitted taxi receipts, I could make enough money to go for a few beers after work. The difference between Metro and taxi fare was about $10. Well worth it.

I went down the stairs and stood near the middle of the platform waiting

for the train. I noticed it stopping before it got to me. I pushed through a few people and saw an elderly lady in a burgundy suit, still holding her purse, standing between the rails in front of the stopped train. I don't know how she got there but she was obviously trying to end her life.

I took a few shots of her looking at the driver still in his seat. The driver climbed down to the track and walked her to the far end of the subway station where paramedics were waiting. What a sad situation.

The train resumed shortly and I went off to the Forum to finish my draft shoot. When I got back to the office I discussed the situation with photo editor Chris Haney. My dilemma was that I had shot pictures at the NHL office and the Metro lady at the same shutter speed on the same role of film. I

needed both sets of photos but how was I going to do it? We decided that I would load about half of the film on a reel, rip it off and load the last part, the part taken at the Metro, on another reel. I would develop the Metro reel about three minutes longer to compensate for the station's low light.

After everything had dried, we looked at the film. I screwed up in one way. I ripped the film in half in the middle of the Metro pictures, but I had ripped it right between two frames. Lucky, yup. There was enough emulsion on all of the Metro negatives.

The photos of the Metro lady got a lot of play across the country. But, I thought it best not to file expenses for a taxi on that assignment.
Doug Ball, Canadian Press

Conservative leader Bob Stanfield fumbles the football – and the election. This photo arguably cost Stanfield the 1974 election.
Doug Ball, Canadian Press

Bob Stanfield's Costly Political Fumble

By Doug Ball

It was the defining photo of Robert Stanfield's political career: knock-kneed, hands clasped awkwardly, grimacing as a football slipped between his bony fingers.

Stanfield's Conservatives were fighting to unseat the minority Liberals of Pierre Trudeau in an election forced by a non-confidence vote. On May 30, 1974, Stanfield's campaign plane touched down for refuelling in North Bay, Ont., midway through a marathon 23 hours of electioneering that took Stanfield and his media posse from Halifax to Vancouver.

It proved to be a fateful 90-minute stop.

Everyone left the plane during refuelling and one of Stanfield's wagonmasters, Brad Chapman, brought out a football to throw around for a little exercise on the tarmac.

I took my motorized Nikon with a 200 mm lens with me just in case. I asked Stanfield if he was going to get in the game, to which he said he might. He was talking with a few people and returned to his conversation. I started playing catch and then noticed Stanfield taking off his jacket.

I stopped playing and picked up my camera. It was always tough to get different pictures of Stanfield. He was a great guy but not photogenic at all. I shot a roll of 36 exposures of him catching, dropping and throwing the ball. I ran into the Air Canada Air Express desk and sent the film to Toronto on the next plane and called the *CP* picture desk to let them know it was coming.

We flew on to a rally in Saskatoon. That night at the airport, I made a quick call to Toronto to see how the photos turned out. Harold Hershell, on the photo desk, said *The Globe and Mail* had Stanfield on the front page but I didn't know which picture.

I rushed on the plane to tell the wagonmaster that he owed me a beer because Stanfield was on the front page of Canada's national newspaper. We laughed and flew on to Vancouver.

CP's picture desk in Toronto had transmitted several photos on the wire. At least one showed Stanfield catching the football. Two others showed him in the act of fumbling a catch, then chasing the errant ball.

Stanfield's catch was not the editor's choice for the front pages of newspapers across Canada.

The next morning, *The Vancouver Province* was under the hotel-room door. I looked at the front page and couldn't believe it. *The Province* ran a two-picture combination of the Tory leader fumbling the football and then running after it. They had even pencilled in his furrowed brow to make it look worse.

I headed downstairs to board the campaign bus to get started on the day's events. I stopped at a newsagent and saw *The Globe and Mail*. They ran one picture of Stanfield fumbling the ball and slugged it, "A Political Fumble?"

I took a seat on the bus and a short time later Southam columnist Charles Lynch sat down in the seat in front of me. He turned around and asked if I had taken the photo of Stanfield that was on the front of *The Globe*.

When I said yes, Lynch said, "Trudeau just won the election."

With voting day still five weeks away, it was hard to argue that the picture would truly cost Stanfield the keys to 24 Sussex Drive.

When Stanfield died in Ottawa on Dec. 16, 2003 at age 89, Bruce Cheadle of *The Canadian Press* wrote a story about the photo and quoted Art Lyon, a lifelong Tory organizer who was working the 1974 campaign.

"I think it came at a particularly bad time, campaigning against Mr. Trudeau, who was perceived by the public as a very athletic guy – flips off diving boards and you name it," Lyon said, adding, "Then all of a sudden there's this one picture of a football and Mr. Stanfield, this crouched-over, bald guy in glasses. Put it this way: it didn't help."

Stanfield already had a reputation for political butterfingers. He'd been accused within his own caucus of letting Lester Pearson's Liberal government off the hook following a non-confidence vote in February 1968. Trudeau then outmanoeuvred Stanfield in the October 1972 elec-

Yes, Stanfield caught some passes... /Doug Ball, Canadian Press

tion. The Tories initially appeared to have one more seat than the Grits but Trudeau maintained a minority government with the support of Ed Broadbent's New Democratic Party.

As Ron Poling, the head of *CP's* picture service, told Cheadle: "He had a reputation for political fumbles and now you've got a picture of him fumbling a football, which really visually stated that. That's the beauty of pictures. They can capture that essence, like a news graphic or a caricature. They can capture the essence, or the time, or the theme, or the perception."

Was it fair comment?

Lyon calls the picture an object lesson for politicians and media alike "because photographers get some stuff that somebody has to make the call about whether it goes out or not. It hit editorially."

There were probably 36 clear negatives of Stanfield on that roll. I didn't edit it but I think I probably would have used the same one.

I was told that at the Press Gallery Dinner following the 1974 election, Stanfield stood and started his speech with this line, "Governor General Léger, Prime Minister, Mr. Broadbent, guests, friends and Doug Ball." As photographers, we were not allowed to be members of the Press Gallery and I only heard this anecdote from someone at Ottawa's *CP* bureau.

Stanfield was a real gentleman. Many years later, in 1988, I got his phone number in Ottawa and called him to see if he and his wife, Anne, would have lunch with me and my wife, Gail, and sign a few of those photographs. I thought I was calling his office but he answered the phone himself. I introduced myself and he paused before saying, "Ah yes, you won an award for that and I got nothing!"

We had lunch in Ottawa a few weeks later and he signed four copies of the famous photo. Afterwards we went outside in a grey, drizzling day to take a few pictures before we parted. Lyon had joined us for lunch and snapped a few of the four of us. When he was finished, Stanfield said, "Just one more, Art. On three, okay?" On three, Stanfield put the hook of his umbrella around my neck and gave me a playful tug and laughed.

He was terrific.

Doug Ball, Canadian Press

...and he could throw as well. /Doug Ball, Canadian Press

Doug Ball, Canadian Press

Grabbing the Moment of Victory

By Lynn Ball

One man's fumble turned into another man's touchdown. I was on vacation haying on my farm near North Gower, Ont., when I was called back to work to cover federal election night, July 8, 1974. It was a thrilling victory for the Grits, giving them a majority victory over Robert Stanfield's Progressive Conservatives (Liberals 141, PCs 95, New Democratic Party 16, Social Credit 11, Independent 1).

For a news photographer trying to get an exciting picture for the front page of *The Ottawa Citizen*, the Liberal celebrations were uneventful. Prime Minister Pierre Trudeau gave his victory speech, accompanied by his wife Margaret, at Ottawa's Chateau Laurier Hotel. I got the usual pictures in both black and white and colour but I had nothing spectacular, nothing that grabbed the moment.

And I didn't have an easy time of it. The black and white pix were shot with a 35 mm Nikon and the colour on a Hasselblad. It was quite a chore, shooting both, as I was loaded down with all of this equipment and using two totally different camera systems. (The quality of the Hasselblad negative in the larger two-and-a-quarter-inch format was preferred for colour.)

Graham Bezant from *The Toronto Star*, Fred Chartrand from *The Canadian Press* and I got talking about what a poor show it was. We decided to drive out to the prime minister's residence, 24 Sussex Drive, to see if Pierre and Margaret were home and try to get a better picture. We walked up to the door of the large stone house and rang the bell. One of the house staff came to the door and I asked if the Trudeaus were home yet. He said no and asked, "What do you want?" I said we would like to get a picture of the victorious Trudeaus being welcomed home by the house staff.

Of course, we were invited in to wait. Who could resist a chance to be photographed with the PM and his wife? The staff had painted a large "CONGRATULATIONS" sign that was hung over the front door. Justin, the Trudeau's first-born son, age two and a half, had pinned on the rose. We got to play with some of Justin's toys while we waited.

Surprised to see us, the Trudeaus asked us what we were doing there. We told them about getting a picture of the house staff welcoming them home, so that was done. Then Pierre said, "You guys put your cameras down and come out on the back porch and have a cold drink." We dropped our cameras and followed Pierre through the house to the screened room overlooking the Ottawa River. Margaret served cold drinks.

We discussed the election for about 20 minutes. After the glasses were empty, Pierre suggested we should go. I had just picked up my cameras by the front door when Margaret locked her arm in Pierre's and suggestively said, "Let's go Pierre, we've got things to do," and gave him a little tug. I grabbed one shot with the super-wide Hasselblad. The CONGRATULATIONS sign was above them and Pierre was in his shirt sleeves.

The next day *The Citizen* ran it huge on Page One.

I went back to the North Gower hayfields. Next week I found out *Time* magazine was going to use it on its cover. This was the election with the famous picture of Robert Stanfield fumbling the football which, some say, cost him victory. I guess if my little brother Doug hadn't taken the picture of Stanfield's fumble, I wouldn't have got this shot of Pierre and Margaret.

The victory photo that made the cover of Time Magazine. /Lynn Ball, Ottawa Citizen

Caesar Paul

By Lynn Ball

Long-lived doesn't mean long-winded or so we found out the day *Citizen* reporter Dave Smithers and I went to Fort Coulonge, Que., to do a story on an Algonquin native who claimed to be 110 years old.

Caesar Paul answered most if not all questions with a simple "yes" and "no", making it hard to obtain any details about his life or the secret to his longevity. I took pictures of him during the interview knowing they were just average and I thought I should be able to get something better.

On leaving, we gave Paul a box of cigars that *The Ottawa Citizen* had sent with us. While I was putting on my coat, I looked back into the living room to see him lighting one up.

I went back in quietly. With available light and a Nikon equipped with an 85 mm 1.8 lens, I captured a pensive Caesar Paul. He was sitting, looking out the window, holding the cigar with 110-year-old parchment skin hands, smoke rising, enjoying his cigar.

The picture, capturing his essence, was used very large in the newspaper. It is one of my favourites. You never know what is going to happen so be ready at all times.

Caesar Paul died in 1975 at age 112.

Lynn Ball, Ottawa Citizen

Mr. Elbows Makes a Joke

By Doug Ball

Two years after the National Hockey League played its 1972 series against the Russians, the World Hockey Association tried to prove to the hockey world that it was as good as the NHL. It played an eight-game series with the Russians, four games in Canada and four in Russia. The WHA was drubbed 7-1 but it was still a great trip for me. I got to see a lot of the world and to hang out a bit with my hero Gordie Howe. He told me one night in Moscow that he had never played such dirty hockey in his life. I mentioned this to other hockey players and they all laughed. Howe knew every dirty trick in hockey, especially the use of his elbows to give himself a bit of room.

J. C. Tremblay, Gordie Howe, Frank Mahovlich and Doug Ball in front of the Kremlin, Moscow, 1974. /Doug Ball, Canadian Press

Waiting for His Prince to Come

By Doug Ball

In late April 1975, Prince Charles toured the Arctic, from east to west including Ellesmere Island, closest Canadian island to the North Pole.

A *Canadian Press* photo editor took a two-week temporary stint with a better-paying Canadian government job to set up darkrooms for the media in towns the Prince of Wales would visit. This ensured that the developer mix was at the right temperature to process the film quickly when the photographers reached the lab. The editor, one of my best buddies for more than 30 years, was Chris Haney, one of the co-inventors of the world famous *Trivial Pursuit* board game.

As we landed at one stop, Haney left on an advance plane to the next one.

At Grise Fiord on Ellesmere Island, Prince Charles headed out with Stuart Hodgson, Commissioner of the Northwest Territories, on sledges pulled by dogs for a private luncheon. Locals who lived in government-built bungalows invited the media to lunch. Trina McQueen of the *Canadian Broadcasting Corporation* was my lunch partner for a feast of muskox stew and bannock bread. McQueen couldn't eat the thin stew of meat, onions and water with salt and pepper. I ate hers as well so the Inuit would know that someone liked their food. It was good. After lunch, I talked to the husband about hunting. I hunt deer and he was impressed that I knew how to handle a 30-06 rifle.

Our final stop was Yellowknife where England's heir to the throne was going for a mile-deep ride in a barrel down a gold mine shaft. I went down first in white coveralls and a hard hat with a light on the front.

A single light bulb helped the miners as they leaned on their drills in a smallish room at the end of the shaft. It was the perfect spot for my hangover – nothing but pain. Water dripped from above as I got ready for Charles's arrival. I found my flash had short-circuited and was useless. I

A miner's lamp lights up Prince Charles deep in a gold mine. /Doug Ball, Canadian Press

tried to shoot some slow shutter speed photos but it wasn't going to work. There wasn't enough light. At the end of the quick visit, I put an 85 mm lens on the Nikon and set it at f1.8 I shone the light on my hat directly on the Prince's face which was spotted with dirt from the drilling. It turned out well and got a lot of play in the newspapers both at home and internationally.

Back at the hotel, the media had decided they were going to give the Prince a gift for such a great trip. Haney and I thought it was bull and shouldn't be done. But someone knew someone who had a narwhal tusk and would have it mounted by the next day.

It was all arranged. Charles would drop by the media room and receive the tusk and visit the photo room before going to dinner. Haney and I were transmitting the first photos ever sent on the Anik satellite and were at work in the lab when the prince was due to arrive.

I had recently bought two new suits of the same pattern, one light brown and the other blue. Haney wore the brown and I was in the blue as we were working sending photos, waiting for our prince to come. Haney, always jumping on ahead, hadn't met Charles and was really looking forward to it. Just as Charles came into the room the phone rang. It was *Canadian Press* head office in Toronto calling. Then the other phone rang. I answered, but they wanted to speak to Haney. He ended up with a phone on each ear and no time to meet with the Prince.

The media all received a pewter mug emblazoned with a Three Plumes medallion from Commissioner Hodgson to commemorate the visit. Except Haney, who didn't get a mug until the millennium year 2000 when we managed to get him one 25 years late. It included a letter from Prince Charles himself.

Chris Haney (left) of The Canadian Press was too busy on the phone to meet Prince Charles.
Bill Ironside, London Free Press

Checkmate in the Window

By Doug Ball

Dr. Henry Morgentaler was on trial at the Palais de Justice in Montreal in 1976 for performing an illegal abortion.

Covering high-profile trials is always a dilemma for us, as taking pictures in the courthouse without permission can lead to contempt of court charges. We can walk around in the building with our camera gear but if a photo appears in a newspaper, we're finished.

Most of the time, we can't get anything because the defendants come in and out another door or through the garage.

One day, at the end of the trial, Dr. Morgentaler came out of the courtroom and walked down to the end of the hall with his brother to wait for the verdict.

There was a great picture right in front of us and we couldn't do anything about it. The Morgentalers were sitting on a window sill playing chess – the game of life – and on the south side of the Palais de Justice.

I had an idea that might work but it depended on how dark the tint was in the building's windows. I left the courthouse through the south door, crossed St. Jacques Street and entered the Olympic Headquarters building. I talked my way upstairs using the name of someone I knew on the Olympic Committee and headed over to the east side of the building.

There was the picture!

From my open window, I could see the Morgentaler brothers playing chess in the Palais de Justice. I put a 200 mm f4 lens on the Nikon and took a lot of pictures at different exposures to compensate for the tinted windows of the courthouse. Lucky for me, at one point the doctor leaned back with his head against the wall behind him and stared up at the sky.

Perfect! Ah yes, a picture's worth a thousand dollars or more!

The Montreal trial was Dr. Morgentaler's third jury trial, resulting again in an acquittal. The Morgentaler story covers a two-decade span beginning in 1967 when Dr. Morgentaler ignited the abortion debate ending with the Supreme Court decision that struck down Canada's abortion law as unconstitutional.

The Morgentaler brothers play chess while waiting for a court verdict. /Doug Ball, Canadian Press

A Picture with a Punch

By Lynn Ball

I have covered only two boxing events in my career and neither was memorable but I managed to get decent pictures at both.

At the Montreal Olympics in 1976 I was on loan from *The Ottawa Citizen* to *The Canadian Press* as part of the National Photo Pool. We were to cover all events with Canadian athletes participating.

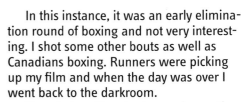

In this instance, it was an early elimination round of boxing and not very interesting. I shot some other bouts as well as Canadians boxing. Runners were picking up my film and when the day was over I went back to the darkroom.

The photo editors had moved an action shot of Filipino Ruben Mares taking a right cross to the face from East German Richard Nowakowski in a featherweight bout. It's a photo you don't plan for as you could never get your timing that good. But the result is spectacular.

As my brother Doug describes it, "The skin is moving but the bones haven't caught up yet."

The shot ran the next day full page on Page One of *The Montreal Star's Olympic Report* and was voted second best picture at the Montreal Olympics.

My other good boxing photo was shot at a local boxing club event in Australia where I was working for the *Morwell Advertiser*, a bi-weekly newspaper.

This picture, one of my favourites, is of a time-out in the corner between rounds. The picture tells the story. The coach has far more enthusiasm than the boxer. It was shot with available light with my old 111F Leica fitted with a Canon 25 mm lens.

Whammo! Two of Lynn's pictures tell the story of life in the ring.
Lynn Ball, Ottawa Citizen; top, Lynn Ball.

This page: A streaker flashes through a crowd of dancers at the Montreal Olympics; Mick Jagger in the crowd. Opposite page: Telly "Kojak" Savalas watches; New Zealand runner John Walker waves to his fans.
Lynn Ball, Ottawa Citizen

Stripped of a Camera during a Streak

By Lynn Ball

I didn't photograph any Canadian gold at the 1976 Montreal Olympics because we didn't win any. Canada didn't do as well as expected and medals were few and far between. Our athletes came up with just five silver and six bronze medals.

For this assignment, I was on loan to *The Canadian Press* by *The Ottawa Citizen* as part of a national pool of photographers to cover Canadian athletes.

Even though I didn't witness Canadian athletes winning gold, I saw Greg Joy win silver in the high jump and was there for some medals awarded in swimming. It was a great experience seeing American Bruce Jenner win the decathalon. Draped in the Stars and Stripes, he ran around the stadium to a cheering crowd and his wife, Kris, came down to kiss and hug him.

I also observed in amazement the East German women's swim team with their manly physiques.

However, the most exciting event for me was the men's 1,500 meter final won by proud New Zealander John Walker. I got a nice shot of him running in the race. My shot of his victory lap waving to the crowd was used full page on the front of the *The Montreal Star's* daily Olympic special section.

My assignment gave me other opportunities to photograph celebrities. For the opening ceremonies in the Olympic Stadium I had the best position in the house, right in front of Queen Elizabeth and Montreal Mayor Jean Drapeau.

I also photographed TV star Telly Savalas, who played the lollipop-sucking New York police lieutenant Theo Kojak, as he made a grand entrance into the stadium to a standing ovation and then left after a few minutes. Mick Jagger and wife, Bianca, made an appearance.

But there was always someone who wanted to spoil our fun. *The Canadian Press* darkroom, which was in a secured area, was broken into one night and only the new equipment was stolen.

And then, during the closing ceremonies in the Olympic Stadium, a streaker ran onto the field at the Big O and danced naked among a

bunch of young girls. He was eventually caught and led away by police. Even though I was in a secure area in front of the VIPs and needed a series of passes and a special numbered bib, someone used the distraction to steal a Hasselblad camera from my camera bag.

After the closing ceremony, I took my film back to the darkroom and the chief of *CP* pictures, Jack Picketts, asked for my bib. I had worn it at both opening and closing ceremonies as well as at all of the athletic events during the games and I was attached to it.

"Okay, give me a minute to take it off."

I went out and locked it in the trunk of my car and I still have it. It is a great souvenir of the 1976 Olympics as only four of these bibs were issued. I didn't think it fair that someone who never wore it in battle was going to end up with it.

Pierre's Pirouette a Gesture of Defiance

By Doug Ball

Pierre Trudeau's famous pirouette behind the Queen may have been a defiant demonstration of his personal independence.

I was covering Trudeau when he attended the G7 Summit Conference in early May 1977 in London, Eng. One of the assignments was to photograph the group of leaders as they headed in for dinner with the Queen at Buckingham Palace. One photographer from each country represented was allowed in. I represented Canada in the photo pool.

Photographers were directed up to the Music Room where the Queen and the heads of the G7 would be coming in from a reception on our left, pose for a few minutes and then head off to our right into the Dining Room.

Finally the doors opened. The Queen was in the middle between Giscard d'Estang of France and U.S. President Jimmy Carter. Prime Minister Trudeau was at the left end so I tried to move down the wall on the left and get closer to him. I was changing lenses, to a 24 mm wide angle, when I looked up and some of the people had started heading off to dinner. Trudeau was still in the same spot looking at his feet. When he looked up he kind of shrugged and did a pirouette before shrugging again and heading off to dinner at the end of the line.

I fired the Nikon the first time without looking through the lens and then shot a few more as he left. I couldn't believe it. What was he thinking about?

The press was escorted out and near the door I threw my film to Bob Dougherty, an *AP* photographer, who ran the film back to the *AP* darkroom at Lancaster House not far from the palace. I hitched a ride with a local photographer to the Hilton Hotel where the rest of the Canadian media was watching the event on television. I spotted *CP* reporter Steve Scott who was working the Summit with me and asked him if he had seen Trudeau doing a pirouette. He said there was nothing on television and burst out laughing when I told him what had happened behind the Queen's back. Scott said the pirouette wouldn't be the lead but would be high up in the story he was about to write.

I headed over to Lancaster House to see my pictures and had plans to meet Scott and the rest of the Canadian media in an hour or so at Wheelers Restaurant. By the time I got there, *AP* was already transmitting the wire photo of Trudeau's pirouette "as he arrives late for dinner." They fished a discarded copy out of the garbage for the press cohort waiting at the restaurant.

At Wheelers, the picture was passed from table to table. Trudeau's press secretary Pat Gossage returned

it to me, saying he intended to show it to Trudeau in the morning. I took it and replied to Gossage that I thought Trudeau would see it anyway.

Two years later I had a chance to talk to Trudeau about the photograph during a refuelling stop in Winnipeg. He looked at my press pass and said, "Oh yeah, you're the guy!!" He said he was in line for the photographs and although he likes the Queen, all the other leaders were trying to get closer for the picture. He held his ground, then did his pirouette. He explained he just "wasn't going to snuggle up to anyone."

Trudeau had come of age in a Quebec where English Canadians ran the economy, and he was committed to social and political change. Each time he stepped onto the international stage, Trudeau gave the impression that he was presenting Canada in a new and exciting light to a watching world. Even his critics liked that.

What other Canadian prime minister would twirl behind the Queen's back?

It reflected an inner strength and independence that was a source of his charisma.

I remember driving on Highway 407 in Brampton, Ont. on Oct. 3, 2000 listening to the radio with tears in my eyes when Justin Trudeau in his eulogy to his father thanked Canadians. "With every card, every rose, every tear, every wave, and every pirouette, you returned his love."

Pierre Trudeau autographed this photo with "and why were we both grabbing at thin air?"/Rod MacIvor

Doug Ball instinctively caught this spontaneous pirouette by Pierre Trudeau. /Doug Ball, Canadian Press

A Heavy Hand Upon My Shoulder

By Doug Ball

In the fall of 1976, after enduring the comedown after the Montreal Olympics summer games, my outlook improved considerably with a call from *The Canadian Press's* head office in Toronto. I was asked to accompany Prime Minister Pierre Trudeau to Japan.

The prime minister's plane stopped in Vancouver to refuel and drop off the Trudeaus' two-year-old son Sacha (Alexandre), who was going to stay the week with his grandparents, James and Kathleen Sinclair, while Mom and Dad were in Asia. There was nothing planned here. I just happened to be in the airport arrivals area as Margaret and Pierre had some fun with Sacha, swinging the little boy between them, as they walked to meet Margaret's parents.

I left the film at the airport with someone from *CP* and carried on with the trip. (When I returned to Canada I found the picture had received a lot of play.)

As we approached Tokyo we were told that we were going on to Osaka because of bad weather. On our arrival at Osaka airport, we were whisked away to the train station and boarded the overnight Bullet Train to Tokyo. It was great, all of us in one rail car.

Margaret and Pierre were asleep. I was three rows up on the other side. This might make a nice photo but I wanted to sneak it. Margaret was wearing a sleeping mask and she was resting her head on her husband's shoulder.

Quietly I set my camera to what I thought the light warranted. I set the mirror to the up position so there wouldn't be any noise. I stood up to go to the toilet and put the camera on my shoulder. On my return, I thought I could turn a little bit one way when I sat back down and shoot the picture then.

Trudeau's head of security, Ralph Coleman, had me figured out. Just before I fired the shutter he put his hand quietly on my shoulder.

"You're not going to take any pictures, are you?"

"No, of course not."

So, as you can see, there is no picture of the Trudeaus on the Bullet Train.

Margaret and Pierre Trudeau playfully swing son Sacha between them at Vancouver airport.
Doug Ball, Canadian Press

Eye-stitched

By Doug Ball

In late 1977, brother Lynn threatened me into taking care of his farm near Ottawa for almost two months while he and his first wife toured Australia.

I had holidays owing plus overtime I could cash in for time off, so we decided that I would move into the farm for the entire time they were away. I did go back to Montreal from time to time but for only a few hours a trip, as I was caring for six polled Herefords. Lynn told me what to feed the cattle and what time, 6 a.m. and 6 p.m.

The day Lynn left for Australia, the cattle were informed of a change in schedule. They would be fed at noon and midnight. After all, I wasn't going to live by their routine. I had more chance of being up by noon and home around midnight.

On one trip to Montreal, I played hockey, my regular weekly game at Lower Canada College arena, the coldest rink in the world. During the game, a guy came up behind me and tried to lift my stick. He missed, carving a nice hole in my cheek just under my right eye.

I finished the game and stopped at the nearest hospital emergency ward on my way back to North Gower. I was on the operating table very quickly with the doctor ready to put in a few stitches. The nurses had placed a sterilized cloth over my face with a small round hole leaving my right eye and the wound exposed. As the doctor began his work, I thought it might make a good picture – my right eye looking down on the work that was going on below.

I always carry a camera with me, so I asked the doctor if he would mind if I took a shot, a close-up. He was interested in photography and agreed immediately.

Focusing the 24 mm lens as close as it would go, I held the camera up near my eye and the cut on my face. I asked the doc to tell me when it was in focus and shot a few photos using natural light. In some frames he was still working away with the sutures.

Eye-stitched got a lot of play in newspapers across Canada and won *The Canadian Press* Feature Picture of the Month and *CP* Feature Picture of the Year.

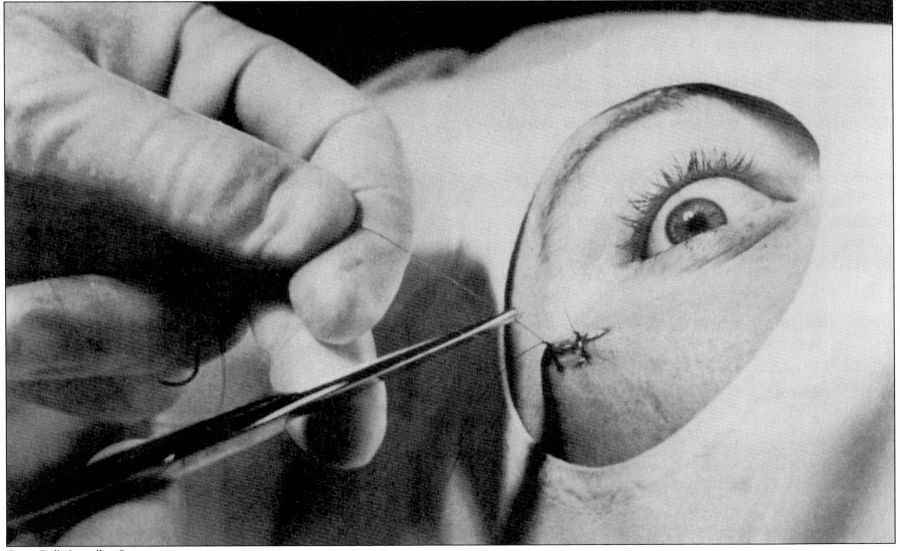

Doug Ball, Canadian Press

The face of sealer Mike Dwyer, streaked in blood, on an ice floe off Newfoundland. /Doug Ball, Canadian Press

The Battle of the Sealers

By Doug Ball

Sealers used three blows with a hakapik to kill seal pups.
Doug Ball, Canadian Press

My part in the 1978 battle between Greenpeace and the sealers on the ice-covered Atlantic Ocean east of Newfoundland and Labrador began right at Gander airport. The weather was vicious but Ed Walters, with the *Canadian Press* office in St. John's, and I set off in a rented car up the Great Western Highway. It was to be a very long day. We were going to St. Anthony on the island's northern tip where the locals were head to head with the protesters, some of them friends and neighbours. After sliding off the road at the famous Gros Morne cliffs, we were stalled until the snowplow stuck ahead of us was pulled out by a second plow. It was dark by the time we arrived in the town, passing the last few kilometres through a white-walled tunnel made by a snow blower.

There was a meeting on the hunt going on at the school so we went directly there. Afterwards we checked into the St. Anthony Motel and I developed my black and white film in the portable darkroom set up in my bathroom. I sent the prints off on the wire and finished the day at the local bar – which happened to be in the motel. Perfect!

The day before the annual hunt was to start, the weather cleared enough for us to fly by helicopter to a fleet of three large vessels at the whelping grounds. Newfoundland Captain Morrissey Johnson invited us aboard the *Lady Johnson II*. Later, we were about to head back to St. Anthony when Johnson, a hospitable, gentle man with flowing white hair and a mustache, invited me to stay for opening day, March 12, 1978.

After a cool night's rest, I woke before dawn to the sound of seal pups calling for their mothers. I was first down the ladder to get shots of the boys leaving the ship to start the harvest. Captain Johnson spoke from the bridge, admonishing one for carrying a baseball bat and made him change to a large ice-pick-like *hakapik*.

"Remember boys, you have to hit the pups three times. First to kill them; second time for the photographers and the third time for the fisheries officer." Johnson was referring to the Canadian federal government's

effort to appease protesters by directing sealers to hit the pups three blows to make sure they were dead before skinning. The seasoned Newfoundlanders knew the seals were dead on the first strike.

Out of a cloudless sky, helicopters carrying Greenpeace members, other media, U.S. Congressman Leo Ryan and actress Pamela Sue Martin came to land near the slaughter. Dressed in a new Greenpeace coat and Sorel boots, Congressman Ryan was heard telling a sealer that he had come to the hunt with an "open mind".

With finger pointing, the "sealer" John Lundrigan, Grand Falls Progressive Conservative member of Newfoundland and Labrador House of Assembly, retaliated, asking Ryan how he could say "open mind" when he had a motion before Congress to condemn the seal hunt.

Later, aboard the *Lady Johnson II*, I shot more pictures in the captain's quarters as Ryan asked Johnson for his opinion on the annual seal hunt at Pribolof Islands off Alaska. "First of all, it's not my country ..." Johnson began. With that, Ryan started looking for his ride off the ice.

I took the helicopter with Walters back to St. Anthony to develop my film. Rushing, I got out five pictures. *CP* was happy with the results so it was time for a few cleansing ales in the motel bar. I ordered a Dominion, a local beer, and settled back to listen to the band.

Progressive Conservative MLA John Lundrigan confronts U.S. Congressman Leo Ryan (right) on the ice during the seal hunt. /Doug Ball, Canadian Press

Captain Morrissey Johnson and guests on the Lady Johnson II.
Doug Ball, Canadian Press

A mother seal protects the skinned body of her pup.
Doug Ball, Canadian Press

I'd hardly begun to relax when a man came over and asked me if I was Doug Ball, the *CP* photographer. He was William Claiborne of *The Washington Post* and *The Los Angeles Times* and had a freelance photographer from New York with him. Would I develop their film and wire some photos to *The Post*? *Associated Press* in New York had given Claiborne my name.

So it was back to my room with five rolls of film. They ended up choosing five pictures and got them ready with captions to wire. I called the

U.S. Congressman Leo Ryan greets a seal up close. /Doug Ball, Canadian Press

U.S. Congressman Leo Ryan passes a bloody carcass. /Doug Ball, Canadian Press

A sealer raises a hakapik to strike a pup. /Doug Ball, Canadian Press

operator to put through a collect call to the *AP* office in Washington. The friendly Gander operator asked my name. I said, "*Canadian Press.*" There was a pause. Then she came back calmly with, "Look, I might be a Newfie but I know your name's not *Canadian Press.*"

Claiborne was grateful for the help but not the photographer. A month later I received a copy of a thank you letter sent to my boss Jack Picketts at *CP* from *The Post* for co-operation shown their paper in an isolated area.

The photographer, a few years later, went off to cover the fighting in Nicaragua. He took a bullet outside the limits of his bulletproof vest and died.

Ryan may have realized that he had taken up a cause that he didn't know enough about. Later that year the politician took up another cause and ended up dead on an airport runway, assassinated on Nov. 18, 1978 at Jonestown, Guyana, by the supporters of Jim Jones.

Johnson, popular at home and made famous by the media coverage of the big-boat seal hunt, was elected Progressive Conservative Member of Parliament for Bonavista-Trinity-Conception in 1984. He lost the seat to Liberal Fred Mifflin in the 1988 election. He died on July 14, 2003, at 70 when a car in which he was a passenger hit a moose and went off the Trans Canada Highway in Central Newfoundland.

Post Script

In the summer of 1978, three Greenpeace protesters from Corner Brook faced two sets of criminal charges for alleged misdeeds during that spring's seal hunt. Rex Weyler, Patrick Moore and Peter Bellem were indicted for loitering in the Department of Fisheries Office and violating the Seal Protection Act, which made it a criminal offence to protect a seal.

Judge Gordon Seabright declared the Crown had failed to prove loitering and dismissed the charges. The protesters who had been hoping to use the trial as a media campaign against sealing were disappointed.

Then the Greenpeace defence team discovered that under a section in Newfoundland's Seal Fisheries Act, it was against the law to kill seals on Sunday. In his first-hand account, published in *GREENPEACE: How a Group of Ecologists, Journalists and Visionaries Changed the World*, (Raincoast Books 2004) Weyler, a Vancouver journalist, writes that upon hearing about the Sunday law, fellow protester Moore declared, grinning:

"They killed seals on Sunday, March 12, the first day we were on the ice. In fact, John Lundrigan, the Newfie cabinet minister, killed seals that day. He was out there getting his mug in front of the cameras and telling how he had just killed 100 seals. He had blood all over him. There are photographs. Doug Ball at *CP* has 'em."

Greenpeacer Bob Hunter had told me, while having a beer at the St. Anthony Motel, "You know we might have screwed up on this one."

On the second round of charges, prosecutor Clyde Wells was able to prove to Judge Seabright's satisfaction that Moore "did minimally interfere with the seal hunt" and he was sentenced to a $200 fine. The minister of justice ignored Greenpeace's appeal and the fine was never paid.

However, the sealing on Sunday charges remain on the books.

Sealers on the ice in front of their ship. /Doug Ball, Canadian Press

René Lévesque and the Wonderbra

By Doug Ball

A premier touring a factory didn't seem like much of a picture opportunity when I was assigned to photograph Quebec's René Lévesque walking through the Dominion Textile plant in Quebec City in late 1978.

It gained promise when I learned it was where they make the Wonderbra.

The tour began with the initial process of constructing the undergarment and continued until we reached mounds of bras stacked on tables. I got some cute shots of Lévesque, whose separatist Parti Québécois Government was elected on Nov. 15, 1976. But Lévesque, rarely without a cigarette, wanted to move on to the prototype room where smoking was permitted.

In the design room, Lévesque lit up and began talking to the company managers. There were a number of manikins wearing different styles of bras. Lévesque asked a boss about a certain model and I took some photos while he smoked and talked business.

Back at the *Canadian Press* office in Quebec City, I developed the film and was delighted by a shot of Lévesque gesturing at a brassiere. It carried possibly the worst caption I have ever written. I slugged the photo "The Finer Points" when I should have written "Let's Talk Separation."

Lévesque and the bra got lots of play. One publication invited people to write in and give it a caption of their own. Some were pretty funny.

Doug Ball says he missed the best caption: Let's talk separation! /Doug Ball, Canadian Press

The Night the Tories Got Their Revenge

By Doug Ball

Joe Clark became leader of the Progressive Conservative Party after Robert Stanfield lost his third attempt to defeat Pierre Elliott Trudeau, less than a year after I got the picture of Stanfield's famous fumble.

We never had a chance at being friends, Clark and me. A few days before the campaign for the May 1979 federal election began, I received a call from Jack Picketts at *The Canadian Press* head office in Toronto. The *CP Pictures* boss told me to be ready to go at any time. He said they had word from "someone" in Ottawa that Joe Clark's PCs didn't want me on their campaign.

This was, he thought, because of my photo of Stanfield dropping a football. I told Picketts that I didn't think it was their call. He suggested that I should get ready for the Conservatives' first flight. Great!

Our first stop on the Clark campaign was an evening rally in Thunder Bay followed by a 9:45 p.m. flight to Toronto to stay the night at the Bristol Place Hotel near the airport. I could leave the rally early and soup my film at the local newspaper in Thunder Bay and transmit my pictures from there. Or I could go downtown after we arrived in Toronto.

On our way to Thunder Bay, Clark worked his way up and down the plane's aisle meeting the media. In turn, I introduced myself. He lit up and said I should have been at an event the week before when he was thrown a football and caught it. It was embarrassing. Later, he signed a campaign photo I took of him wearing a toque.

I decided the only way to make the morning papers was to leave the rally early and then go straight to the airport from the newspaper. I told *CP*'s reporter Paul Gessell my plans. I photographed Clark's arrival at the rally, shaking hands as he passed through a cheering crowd. I took a few pictures of him delivering his speech.

I did my work and the managing editor of *The Chronicle-Journal* drove me to the airport. There was an Air Canada DC 9 lifting off as we pulled in just after 9:30 p.m. We went into the terminal and I saw another Air Canada DC 9 on the tarmac so figured that was our plane and the media bus hadn't arrived at the airport.

Well, I was wrong. It happened that during Clark's speech the PC wagonmaster went to the media and told them our plane was leaving 15 minutes earlier than planned. Nobody had told me. I booked myself on the next flight at 7 a.m. and checked into a hotel. No change of clothes. No toothbrush. No comb. All I had was my camera gear.

When I arrived in Toronto, I gave a cabbie $10 to get me quickly to the Bristol Place Hotel. I got there just as everyone was boarding the campaign bus for the day's trip to Kitchener. My bag was sitting in the lobby so I threw it back on the bus.

The day was spent in the same clothes. Do you think the PCs got what they wanted?

Conservative leader Joe Clark demonstrates why politicians should never wear a toque. /Doug Ball, Canadian Press

Whining and Pleading Paid Off

By Doug Ball

In May 1975 I was sent to cover the finals of the AVCO Cup, symbolic of the championship of the World Hockey Association, in Quebec City. The Houston Aeros were playing off against the Quebec Nordiques.

It turned out to be the final game and the Aeros were going to win so I headed downstairs behind the players from the Aeros who were ready to go on the ice to celebrate their win. I was pushed in behind the bench with my hero, Gordie Howe, right in front of me.

Just before the buzzer went I noticed someone moving in from the right. It was his son, Mark, who put his arm around his dad and his head on his shoulder. I'm sure I pushed someone over behind me as I backed up to get a photo of a family affair.

I sent four other pictures that night on the wire, then asked if I could send a nice feature picture of a kid with his head on his dad's shoulder. The photo editor said that he had enough photos of the event but when I protested, he said I could send one more. *The Ottawa Citizen* ran the picture almost a full page the following day ... it was worth the argument !

Doug Ball, Canadian Press

Through the Habs' Window

By Doug Ball

Bernard "Boom Boom" Geoffrion, a 50-goal scorer (1961) for the Montreal Canadiens, signed as The Habs head coach on Sept. 20, 1979 with great fanfare.

Thirty games into the season the team had a dismal record. Something had to be done.

On the evening of Dec. 12, we received a tip at *The Canadian Press* Montreal office that something was happening at the Canadiens' headquarters at the Montreal Forum on Closse Street.

I found the doors to the offices locked but the lights were on upstairs. I ran into Mike Dugas, a respected photographer with *The Montreal Gazette.* We knew Geoffrion was inside and he might be fired or resign.

I had a 500 mm Nikon mirror lens in my camera bag so Dugas and I made a deal agreeing to share any pictures we got. I went across the street to the Texas Restaurant and managed to talk my way onto their roof. Up there, it was pitch dark. I stumbled my way across the flat roof until I could see into the hockey team's windows.

Geoffrion walked by the window and then I saw Irving Grundman, Canadiens' managing director. I found an air conditioning unit that wasn't turned on – it was Montreal in December – so I could rest my camera. With that long lens, I knew I would have to shoot at a 30th of a second at f8 and 800 asa.

Finally the two of them were visible in one window with Geoffrion facing my way. I fired off a bunch of frames to be sure that I had at least one fit to print.

Shortly afterwards someone came over to the window, looked over at me and closed the curtains.

I rushed down to meet Dugas standing guard at The Habs' entrance. We staked out the doors to the executive suites a while longer but, with deadlines looming, left to make the morning papers.

We made the fronts of the sports sections across the country. What a feeling!

The gloom on Boom Boom Geoffrion's face in the window told the story of his firing. /Doug Ball, Canadian Press

Tory chief John Diefenbaker railed against those who would depose him, especially Dalton Camp (opposite page, with Robert Stanfield). /Lynn Ball, Ottawa Citizen

Saved from the Bell

By Doug Ball

My brother Lynn and I were in direct competition on the Diefenbaker funeral train and at one Prairie stop I had to scramble to keep up.

John George Diefenbaker, prime minister of Canada from 1957 to 1963, died at his home in Ottawa on Aug. 16, 1979. He had made extensive plans for his funeral including a two-day train trip to Saskatoon. There the Progressive Conservative leader was laid to rest on the grounds of the University of Saskatoon close to a building named after him, the Right Honourable John G. Diefenbaker Centre.

One of the cars on the Diefenbaker train was filled with journalists including four photographers: Boris Spremo for *The Toronto Star*. Denis Paquin for *United Press Canada* international wire service, Lynn for *The Ottawa Citizen* and myself for *The Canadian Press* news co-operative. We departed from Ottawa for the prairies on Aug. 19.

With many whistle stops ahead, we reflected on Diefenbaker's wish that it be a "dry" run, no alcohol on board. Lynn didn't mind – he doesn't drink. But as the train jerked into motion we thought we heard the sound of wine corks popping in the steward section. Sure enough, it wasn't a "dry" train.

As we went to bed on the second night, we knew we would be making a quick stop in Melville, Sask., at 6 a.m. I got up as the train was slowing down and ran into Lynn while I was getting off to take photographs of the locals viewing the flag-draped casket.

The casket carried both the Canadian flag and Diefenbaker's much-preferred Red Ensign. As the train stopped in each small place enroute to Saskatoon, some officers with the Royal Canadian Mounted Police would slide open the doors of the funeral car and Canadians could have a moment with a beloved former prime minister. At some of the stops someone with the Diefenbaker entourage would say a few words of thanks.

This time as the doors opened an elderly man standing in front of us dropped to the ground gasping for air. I jumped down beside him and tried to help him. The Mounties took over and began CPR, cardiopulmonary resuscitation.

Being photographers, we had to do our jobs. We started shooting pictures of the man and his helpers with the Diefenbaker casket in the background. A few minutes later an ambulance arrived and the man was whisked away but we heard later he didn't make it. As the ambulance pulled away, I looked down the line of cars and there was one of our fellow photogs running towards us. He missed the shot; the other one slept through everything.

Back on the train, we were heading to Watrous two hours away. Lynn and I jerry-rigged a darkroom in the news car's restroom. We put the film into a black bag and put it in the developing tank. We taped plastic garbage bags over the bathroom windows and made prints. We had to make quite a few because the train shaking the enlarger made most of them unusable. We finally succeeded and wrote captions for the best photos. Lynn was trying to make *The Citizen*'s afternoon edition. I was trying to send mine to *CP Toronto* so they could release it nationally. It takes eight minutes to send a photo on the telephone wire and we had only a 10-minute stop in Watrous.

There was only one public phone at the Watrous train station and, without telling me, brother Lynn had reserved it for himself. So much for brotherly love. When the train stopped Lynn went into the station. I ran across a dirt road to a gas station and asked the guy if I could use his phone to send a picture to Toronto. You can guess the look on his face! He agreed but the service bell rang and he had to go out and pump gas.

To send a picture by phone in those days, we would take the cover off the mouthpiece, hook up two alligator clips from the transmitter and send the print. I looked for the phone and found it was a Princess, a flat one. You can't unscrew its mouthpiece. I had to hook the photo transmitter to the wall outlet. That meant the mouthpiece was still live but I couldn't have other noise going down the line. It would ruin the photo.

I paid the guy $5 to stand outside and not let anyone cross the hose that rang the bell in the office. I held the train up for a few minutes but it was worth it.

Winter Olympics Assignment was a Miracle on Film

By Doug Ball

In early 1980, I drove down to Lake Placid, N.Y., from Montreal to cover the Winter Olympics. I would witness a miracle.

The Canadian Press news co-operative works with *The Associated Press* so I could transmit my photos through the *AP* media centre set up in the town's high school beside the outdoor speed skating rink and the Olympic arena. Some of the other venues were miles away and I worried about trying to cover everything. I could pick photos from *AP* but I had go through the negatives to find Canadian content.

Some days, I climbed on a bus and went to the bobsled run, biathlon and other stirring sites. There was no hockey for the first few days but it started soon enough. It was fantastic. The day after the first Canadian game, I was called into the *AP* photo boss's office. He'd been talking to Jack Picketts, *CP* picture chief in Toronto.

I thought I must have screwed up something. He said he had asked *CP* if he could take me off the other events to shoot only hockey and *AP* would cover for me. Covering hockey was OK by me!

I had a spot above the lower section at centre ice, a 400 mm lens on the Nikon and a film runner. Life couldn't get any better.

The U.S. beating the Soviet Union 4-3 on Feb. 22, 1980 is one of my top memories of any Olympic Games.

The USSR had won the last four Olympic gold medals and clobbered the U.S. 10-3 a few days before the Lake Placid Olympics began. The U.S. team of 20 mostly college players was considered a long shot to win any medal at the Games.

The U.S. team went on to beat Finland to win the gold medal. Their victory is credited for the growth of hockey in the United States and the world. Thirteen of the 20 American players went on to play in the National Hockey League. Captain Mike Eruzione did not but in 2004, when the movie *Miracle* came out, he had 110 public speaking engagements to talk about the 1980 team.

Glenn Anderson attempts to score on Alexander Tretiak the Soviet netminder. /Doug Ball, Canadian Press

No Commie Sweater for Bobby Clarke

By Doug Ball

Putting on Czech sweaters are Steve Shutt, Bobby Orr and Bob Gainey. /Doug Ball, Canadian Press

The first Canada Cup final game in 1976 was at the Montreal Forum with Canada playing the Czechs. It was the first time Bobby Orr had played in an international tournament. The game ended in a tie but Darryl Sittler scored in the first overtime period for the victory.

The teams lined up on their blue lines and the players traded sweaters with the other team. Prime Minister Pierre Trudeau presented the Canada Cup Trophy to Team Canada captain Bobby Clarke, who was not wearing the Czech sweater he had traded with the other team. He didn't want to put on a Commie sweater after playing against a Communist country in 1972, he said.

After the presentation, Clarke skated around the Forum holding a large Canadian flag with members of the winning team following. Left to right, Bobby Clarke, Denis Potvin, Marcel Dionne, Guy LaPointe, Darryl Sittler, Peter Mahovlich and Lanny McDonald. Bobby Hull and Bobby Orr told me recently that it was the best hockey team ever! */Doug Ball, Canadian Press*

Super sleuth Doug Ball tracked down Prime Minister Pierre Trudeau skiing in the Alps near Innsbruck. /Doug Ball, Canadian Press

If Only I'd Taken My Skis!

By Doug Ball

It was close to Christmas 1980, when I got a call from Jack Picketts at *The Canadian Press* news co-operative head office in Toronto. Prime Minister Pierre Trudeau was going on a global tour of six countries. Beginning in Austria, he would visit Algeria, Nigeria, Senegal, Brazil and Mexico over two weeks in January.

The media was scheduled to leave Ottawa around Jan. 5 and pick up the PM in Salzburg after his week's holiday at an undisclosed Austrian ski resort. Picketts wanted me to fly over early and find the Liberal leader while he was still on vacation. It sounded like fun to me!

Shortly after Christmas Day, I was off to Europe. In Munich, I boarded the Orient Express to Salzburg and booked into a hotel. Next day, with the help of an editor at a local newspaper, I tracked down Trudeau at the Post Hotel in Lech, north of St. Anton, not far from Innsbruck. I could take a train to St. Anton, a couple of hours away, and then a bus up to Lech.

I left the next day, keeping my room in Salzburg as I had a black and white and colour portable darkroom and a transmitter with me. I thought that being near a friendly newspaper was a good idea. There wasn't a hard deadline on these photos. The competition wouldn't start until the photog from *United Press International* joined the press tour from Ottawa.

Arriving in Lech in the afternoon, a postcard of mountains surrounding a village with a river running through it, I found the Post Hotel and went looking for a room for me. Nothing available, was the hoteliers' constant response. "Busiest time of the year." After the sun went down, I was still looking for a place to stay, but "nothing," they all said.

I was walking on Lech's beautiful main street by the river when I noticed two men coming towards me. One was wearing a fur hat like one Trudeau wore. Walking closer to the street, he was dwarfed by his companion. I tilted my head away slightly as they passed. It was the PM for sure.

They headed into a restaurant and I kept looking for a room. I didn't want to tip my hand before I had fired off a few frames. I finally took a taxi to St. Anton as the buses had stopped running by then. All the hotels there had the same answer. "No vacancy." I found a discothèque that stayed open most of the night and asked the bouncer in German if he spoke English.

"No worries, mate."

He was an Aussie working his way around the world. He had only a little room where he and his girlfriend stayed but he did have a snow-bound Volkswagen bus and a couple of sleeping bags that I could sleep in. He took me out to the bus, cleared off some snow and unlocked the door. Wow, I could finally lie down and stretch out. It was like the Ritz! He kept the key and asked me to lock the door when I left in the morning. I thanked him and went to sleep.

I woke up in time to make the bus back to Lech, but not before getting a souvenir shot of the van. At the Post Hotel I asked if Trudeau had left for the slopes. It was about 9 a.m. He was still having breakfast, the desk clerk said. I noticed a tall man turn and walk towards me. I thought it might be security. It was a Royal Canadian Mounted Police officer. He introduced himself and asked who I was. I told him and he seemed okay with that but said he would have to warn the PM that I was here before he came down. I didn't really give a shit after what I'd been through the last few days.

I waited outside with my camera ready to fire off a few frames if they stopped me from following Trudeau. I didn't know the rules in Austria. Anyway, it was no big deal. I stood there in the brown ski jacket my wife Gail had given me for Christmas and my new toque with ski goggles on top of it, and enjoyed the nice sunny morning, a great day to ski.

There was no room in the inn, so Doug snuggled down in this snowbound van. /Doug Ball, Canadian Press

Pierre Trudeau gives ski-less Doug a big smile as he takes to the hills. /Doug Ball, Canadian Press

Press secretary Pat Gossage shows a picture of Trudeau skiing to journalists gathered in a press briefing. /Doug Ball, Canadian Press

Finally Trudeau emerged with two other guys I didn't know. He looked over and said, "Oh, it's you." Immediately I felt better. "Where are your skis?"

I took a few frames before he got close enough to really talk. I said I didn't have any skis but I was assigned to get some shots of him skiing for *The Canadian Press.* He suggested I go across the river and up the hill past the last chalet. He offered to take the chairlift to a place just above that and he would ski down towards me. Then he could take off and so could I.

"Is he really going to do that or is he giving me the runaround?" I thought as I puffed my way over the bridge and up the mountain.

Sure enough, down he came with the two guys behind him. I took some action shots of him turning on skis towards me and then some wide angle still shots with the village behind him. Beautiful. He said thank you and see you later.

I got the next bus to St. Anton and the next train to Salzburg. At a train stop near my destination, I took a picture of the station clock as it passed midnight. I'd almost forgotten it was New Year's. I celebrated by peeling an orange.

In my room, I developed the film and dried it. I tried to make a print but the little Durst enlarger wouldn't produce enough light to make

an exposure on the photo paper. I wrapped some black plastic around my Vivitar flash and printed the Trudeau pictures that way. Whatever works!

It took several hours to transmit the photos to Toronto. At one point, the assistant manager knocked on my door because my phone bill was already $900 U.S.

A couple of days later, I headed back to Lech to get some more photographs of the holidaying PM, maybe some in colour. At St. Anton they wouldn't let me on the bus. The road had been covered by an avalanche and wouldn't reopen for days. The 22 frames I had would have to do.

The plane with the Ottawa media arrived a day later, but no Trudeau. He was snowbound by the blocked road and fog. The helicopters couldn't land in Lech.

Still, we managed a press conference by telephone. The reporters plugged their tape recorders into a box at the front of the room connected to a phone in Trudeau's room in Lech. The reporters asked him if being stuck in Lech was a hardship.

"It is very tough here," he said. "As a matter of fact, today we ran out of avocado and shrimp."

My pictures of Trudeau skiing made front pages all over.

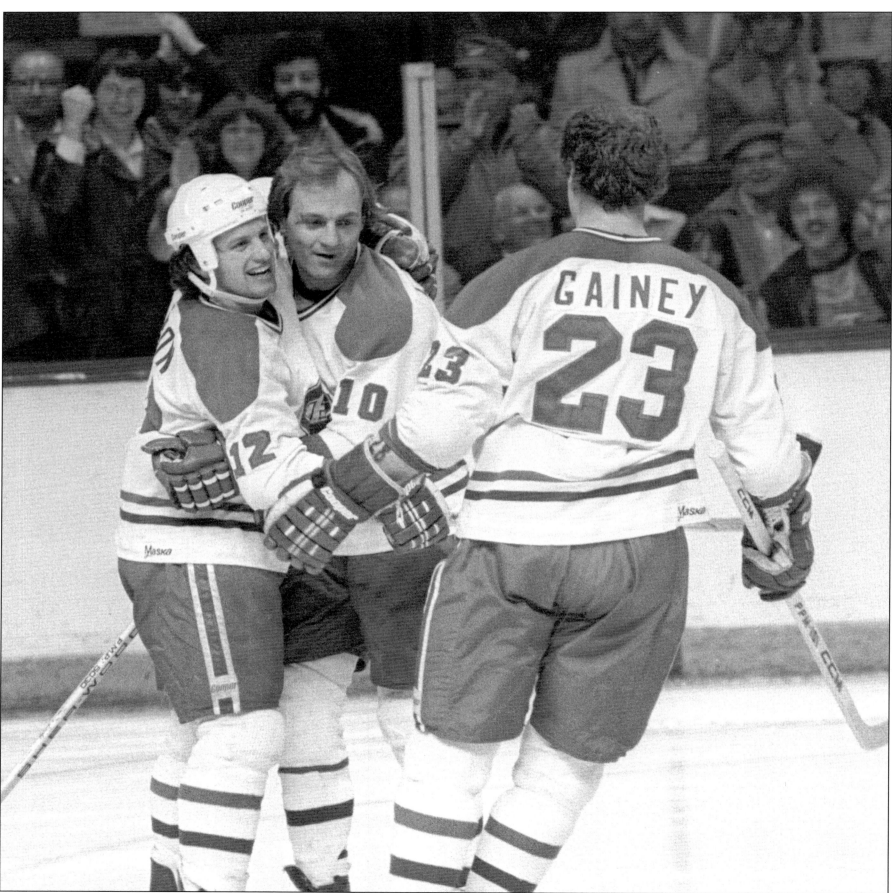

Bob Gainey and Keith Acton congratulate Guy Lafleur on reaching his 1000-point milestone. /Doug Ball, Canadian Press

Lafleur Scores 1000th Point

By Doug Ball

As a photographer for *The Canadian Press* office in Montreal, part of my job was covering the fabled Montreal Canadiens, aka The Habs, The Bleu Blanc Rouge – the best hockey team of all time.

Heading out to the Forum to cover a game was never boring. Most of the time it was my first meal of the day, sometimes the only one. If you covered sports, hockey, football, baseball and soccer, you could eat all year for nothing.

The photogs' room meals were not as good as the reporters' room stuff but we had nicer people. The photogs were served small square sandwiches with the crusts cut off and they were always fresh. They also had steamed hotdogs as only Montrealers can make them. The appliance has the buns in one side and the wieners in the other so they're never soggy.

As I ate my meal, washed down with a cold Molson, I'd read the prepared press notes on the two teams playing that night. I figured it was always better to have a picture that might match a story than just an action shot.

On March 4, 1981, the Canadiens were playing the Winnipeg Jets. Someone told me that competitor *United Press Canada* was using a rookie freelance photographer and he had been told to keep his eye on me. He was also told to get back to the office and put a picture on the wire by 10 p.m.

This would be fun, I thought. After the first period we usually headed off for the office to make the deadlines of the morning papers. Tonight the press notes showed that Guy Lafleur had 997 points to date. To add more interest, Lafleur had notched two points in the first period!

I knew I had to stay. But I put on my coat when I got back to the photographers' room after the first period. I glanced over and saw the young *UPC* photog was watching me. He put on his coat. A few minutes passed and I took off my coat, walked over to the fridge and took out a beer. He took off his coat but kept looking at his watch. Soon he put on his coat and left the building.

I was a little late to make the morning papers but my photos were used all over Canada, even in the local Quebec newspapers. I had Lafleur being handed the puck by teammate Larry Robinson and Lafleur smiling at teammate Keith Acton after scoring his 21st goal of the season in the third period. It was his 1000th point in his National Hockey League career.

Ryan Remiorz, *UPC's* photographer that night, is now a very good friend and tells this story on himself. Remiorz is a National Newspaper Award winning photographer for *The Canadian Press* in Montreal.

Larry Robinson hands Guy Lafleur the puck that scored his 1000th point. /Doug Ball, Canadian Press

New Democratic Party leader Ed Broadbent, flanked by armed guards, scrambles from an armoured van in San Salvador in 1981. /Doug Ball, Canadian Press

Just Broadbent and Me and President Duarte

By Doug Ball

In May 1981, I learned how people play politics at the point of a gun. I was assigned to go to Central America with Ed Broadbent, leader of the New Democratic Party. Our first stop was Mexico City, through Miami, and there the agenda began to change. Former NDP leader David Lewis died that day and Broadbent headed back to Canada for the funeral. That was tough, spending a couple of days in Mexico on expenses, waiting for his return.

When we arrived at San Salvador, El Salvador, the picture got uglier. Unlike the other passengers, we were taken off the plane onto the tarmac where an armoured van waited for us. A few guys in jeans were standing around and I thought they worked at the airport, until I saw the guns sticking out of their belts.

They were our guards, it turned out. We hopped into the van. I was a little scared but Broadbent was well under control. The driver and a guard sat in front. Douglas Sirrs, Canadian ambassador to Costa Rica, Nicaragua, Honduras, El Salvador and Panama, and myself sat behind them. Broadbent and a translator were in the third seat. Two more guards with machine guns faced backwards in the last seat.

The windows of the van had darkened bulletproof windows added on the inside over four centimetres (1.5 inches) thick. The guard in the front seat pointed out the place in the road where a few months earlier four nuns had been killed. We were stopped a number of times as we headed into San Salvador. The driver slowed down and checked along the rivers and creeks going under the road, and I guessed that was because it might be a great place for a bomb.

Broadbent met first with the Papal Nuncio of the Holy See, during which I got a phone call through to Steve Scott at *Canadian Press* in Ottawa. I told him about the planned visits and the armed guards. Then I did a few minutes of voice stuff for *Broadcast News*.

Our next stop was a visit to a vicar in San Salvador but I was not allowed to take pictures. As we waited outside, I showed our four guards pictures of my newborn son. I figured they couldn't shoot anyone who had young kids.

Broadbent meeting with El Salvador President Duarte. /Doug Ball, Canadian Press

It was decided we wouldn't go on to Costa Rica after all, but rather return to Mexico City. Then we got word we were to meet with El Salvador President José Napoleon Duarte in the Presidential Palace. We were escorted into his office – just Broadbent and me. Afterwards we flew back to the airport in a helicopter arranged by Duarte – flying at treetop level to give shooters on the ground less time to aim. (That's the most frightened I've been on any assignment.)

When we got to the San Salvador airport, we didn't have any tickets to go back to Mexico City. I threw down my VISA card and bought tickets for everyone.

In Cuba, after El Salvador, we got nothing. Expecting we would be going to a meeting with President Fidel Castro after lunch at the Canadian embassy, we enjoyed the hospitality. Then our party headed out in two cars to meet Castro. At a fork in the road, the lead car with Broadbent went right and the second car, with us in it, went back to our hotel.

When they dumped us at the hotel, I decided to head out to find the place where Broadbent was meeting with Castro. All of a sudden a bunch of Cuban police started to follow me out of the hotel. I gave up and went back inside.

The only good thing about the trip to Cuba was a box of Montecristo #3 cigars for $52. Wow!

Doug rides in the front seat of a treetop level helicopter ride back to the airport, arranged by President Duarte. /Doug Ball, Canadian Press

Queen Elizabeth II and Prince Philip make their way down Fleet Street on their way to the wedding of Prince Charles. /Lynn Ball, Ottawa Citizen

The Best Wedding Coverage of All

By Lynn Ball

I heard on the car radio that Prince Charles was getting married on July 29, 1981, to Lady Diana Spencer. The next day I went in to talk to Russ Mills, the editor of *The Ottawa Citizen*. I suggested that *The Citizen* run a special wedding supplement of the future king, full of adverts, and I would go to London and photograph the event so we would have *Citizen* exclusive photos.

"I'll get back to you," said Mills, a thoughtful and unhurried man, respected by his colleagues.

A few days later he called me into his office and said *The Citizen* would be doing a royal wedding special edition and I was going to photograph the event. I phoned Buckingham Palace and secured accreditation and after a few calls reserved a rooftop position five storeys up and across the street from St. Paul's Cathedral where the nuptials would take place.

As part of the wedding coverage promotion, the newspaper carried out a fashion makeover on Chris Cobb and Michael Prentice, both seasoned journalists originally from the U.K., and myself to show readers how one should dress for a royal wedding. The story and pictures ran on a fashion section front. We were subjected to hairdos in a beauty salon, fancy clothes and shoes that we would never have worn by choice.

I ended up looking like a pimp in white pants, a bright red jacket and pouffed up hair. In London, the news desk called and asked me to get a picture taken of the three of us in front of St. Paul's Cathedral. I did this and sent it back to Ottawa only to have the desk call back asking for one in our wedding clothes. The makeover story did say we would be wearing them but they weren't given to us. Even the news desk was fooled.

One night the three of us went out to a Soho basement restaurant. Prentice needed cigarettes and was told he could get some upstairs in the bar. He was gone a long time and when he came back he was very upset and angry. It seems he put his money into a cigarette machine and no cigarettes came out. Management wouldn't give his money back and threw him out of the bar. Now Prentice wanted us to join him in beating them up and getting his money back. Cobb and I finally got him calmed down and we had supper.

The Citizen
Royal Wedding
Souvenir Edition

The Citizen, Ottawa, Thursday, July 30, 1981, Page 33

From London ...with love

The Prince and Princess of Wales are dwarfed by the massive pillars of St. Paul's Cathedral as they emerge after their wedding ceremony

Lynn Ball, Citizen

Fairy tales can come true . . .

In the end, it was about love. After the procession of processions, and with massed choirs and fanfares to salute them, two people stood before the world and declared their love.

Charles, a 32-year-old man of the world, a man of titles — Prince of Wales, Earl of Chester, Baron Renfrew, Lord of the Isles, Great Steward of Scotland, Order of the Garter and Order of Bath — took a wife. A princess.

His bride — a radiant, yet shy, 20-year-old kindergarten teacher of noble birth, Lady Diana Spencer, who became Princess of Wales.

A man born to be King turned to his God and made solemn vows, with words such as love and honor.

His chosen princess returned those vows, and held his hand firmly as they spoke the words, "I will," and the choirs sang out:

O let the nations rejoice and be glad!

When it was over, they touched, then kissed.

It was, as the archbishop who married them said: "The stuff of which fairy tales are made."

On leaving the restaurant, Prentice spotted, through the bar's front window, the guys who had thrown him out. He started pounding on the glass, making obscene gestures. Cobb and I quickly hauled him off before we got into a street fight in Soho. It is good to report that Prentice, now a pensioner, is very sedate and respectable.

I had to find a way to get to Heathrow airport right after the wedding so I did a test run on the subway and by taxi. The subway was faster but that was to change at the last minute. The evening before the wedding Prince Charles was speaking in Hyde Park so I went over to take a look.

I could hear his voice on the loud speakers that were set up but I couldn't find him in the vast crowd of 600,000 people jamming the streets, more than the entire population of Ottawa. Afterwards they all lined up for the Tube. It was like bathwater trying to go down a plugged drain.

I couldn't use the Tube to get to the airport after the wedding, it would probably be plugged. A couple of days earlier, a taxi driver had given me his card saying if I needed anything just give him a call. I called him, got him out of bed and explained the situation. He said to meet him on Blackfriars Bridge, the bridge closest to St. Paul's, and he'd meet me on the far side, as most of the bridges would be closed.

I was now counting on him. I didn't get to bed until very late and had to be up quite early to get into position on the rooftop opposite the cathedral.

Attendees carefully arrange the long train of Diana's wedding dress outside St. Paul's Cathedral. /Lynn Ball, Ottawa Citizen

It was a great position to shoot from, a wonderful view. It was a little high, but the entire area in front of the church was visible and from the other side I could see straight down Fleet Street from where the carriages and the wedding party would be coming.

The weather was fantastic. I was loaded with equipment. Nikon had loaned me a 400 mm 2.8 lens with a 2X converter making it an 800 mm 5.6. I had that lens on a 3F Nikon camera mounted on a tripod aimed at the front of the cathedral. I also had another F3 Nikon with a 300 mm 2.8 and an F2 Nikon with a 180 mm lens plus a few shorter lenses and another camera body or two including an old F.

The guests were now beginning to arrive including Prime Minister Pierre Trudeau and Governor General Edward Shreyer. Then the wedding party with Queen Elizabeth II and Prince Philip in an open carriage came down Fleet Street with the pomp and ceremony that could only happen at a wedding of a future king.

Prince Charles, a 32-year-old man of titles, arrived and, as he entered the cathedral, he turned and gave a quick wave and smile to the crowds. Then Diana, a demure 20, in her spectacular gown arrived in the fairy tale glass coach with her father, Earl Spencer. She was all the way up the stairs before the train of her dress made it out of the coach. It was 25 feet long.

Prince Charles and Princess Diana leaving St. Paul's. /Lynn Ball, Ottawa Citizen

Finally everyone was in St. Paul's and it was quiet outside. I sat down, soaked in sweat. I was exhausted. The intensity of the concentration needed to take the photographs was draining and I needed a few minutes to recover.

I had a smile on my face because I knew I had the pictures that I wanted and needed and all that was left was to get the couple coming out of the church. The pressure was off and the final pictures would be taken with an easier feeling. I was ready with the 800 mm when the royal newlyweds emerged; I took a few frames then quickly picked up the 300 mm for a few more wide shots before they got to their carriage. The 300 mm was like a wide angle, I was that far away. It worked out well as the 800 mm shot was used on Page One and the wider shot taken with the 300 mm filled the entire front of the special supplement.

After the Prince and Princess of Wales disappeared down Fleet Street, I packed my gear and headed for Blackfriars Bridge. I was loaded down with equipment like a packhorse. I hurried down the streets and made it to the bridge totally done in. As I started across the bridge, I saw the taxi driver. He spotted me and came and took some of my camera gear.

In the cab, he said we had time to stop for a drink before I had to be at the airport. When we got out of the main part of London he pulled into a pub. I don't drink alcohol but I needed some liquids, I'd been hours

without any. I pointed to a pint beer mug, "Put some ice in that and start opening those little bottles of tonic water and keep pouring them in until it's full," I said to the bartender.

Man was that good, the most refreshing drink I have ever had.

Things went smoothly at Heathrow and I was in Ottawa that evening well before deadline. The time difference was on our side. The rest is *Citizen* history.

We had, in my opinion and in that of many others, including the bosses, the best royal wedding newspaper coverage in Canada. The wedding took place before a congregation of 3,500 and a global TV audience of 750 million. Readers loved the Souvenir Edition and, for years after, people I met along the way praised the pictures.

That was in the days before digital photography and digital transmission of photographs. The old method of sending colour photographs over the wire made it difficult to get good reproduction in the newspaper. This was why it was essential to get the original film back for maximum printing quality in the newspaper.

The Citizen liked to have exclusive coverage of news events. That made it difficult but exciting and challenging for a photographer because you were expected to get pictures as good or better than any available. *Citizen* editors also liked to use a picture from a different angle even though other dailies would use the same pictures as other newspapers.

After the planning and hard work, it is great to see it all in print.

An 800 mm lens zeroed in on the royal couple. /Lynn Ball, Ottawa Citizen

A bear cub howls as a Ministry of Natural Resources biologist prepares to check his weight. /Lynn Ball, Ottawa Citizen

Bear with Me for a Moment

By Lynn Ball

A bear's den is an extremely cramped space for a Momma bear, two cubs ... and a photographer.

In mid-March 1982, I got an invitation from Stuart Strathearn of the Ministry of Natural Resources office in North Bay to go along on a survey of hibernating female black bears to count cubs and to take blood samples and measurements. The bears were wearing radio collars so they could be tracked down easily.

I'd been on a similar study with Strathearn a year earlier. That time I was photographing technicians preparing to enter a den when I noticed two paws followed by a snout emerging from a hole in the ground about a foot away from my foot.

"There's your bear," I called out, taking off at a run.

One of the men grabbed a shovel used to dig out the den's entrance and placed it gently on the bear's head, pushing its head back down into the hole. The bear retreated and went back to sleep. Then it was drugged, removed from its den and examined.

This adult bear was drugged before being measured but its cub was conscious and yowling while being weighed (above, right). /Lynn Ball, Ottawa Citizen

This time, the den was close to the highway and not far from some houses at Redbridge, Ont., just outside North Bay. One of the technicians had his two children with him. The kids would keep the bear cubs warm under their jackets while their mother was examined. The doorway was dug out and Momma was tranquilized with a needle mounted on the end of a stick long enough to reach the sleeping bear. After a short wait to ensure Momma was out, Strathearn wiggled into the den.

When he came out, he said there were cubs in the den and asked me if I wanted to go in and photograph them. "Sure thing," I said. In I went. A bear's den is a very tight fit. There's not much room to move about. When I got down to the bears it was totally dark. If I moved to one side, a little light got in around me. I could feel and just make out some of Momma, and I could hear the cubs awake on the far side of her but I couldn't see them.

I had to crawl over her and it was a very tight squeeze. As I began crawling over her body, she let out a loud moaning growl. I don't know how I did it but I shot like a rocket backwards out of the hole.

I went back in and this time was able to move the twins to Momma's near side. It was exciting photographing cubs in a den next to a large sleeping bear. I didn't do this every day.

I crawled out and brushed off the dirt while the technicians did their work. The cubs howled loudly when they were dangled by one foot from the scales. Each weighed about two kilograms and had large paws and claws. Snuggled in the children's jackets they settled down while Momma did her part for science. She was pulled out of the den while they replaced the batteries in her radio collar, measured, weighed, pulled a tooth and took a blood sample.

The threesome was then put back in their den and the entrance was covered with branches and snow while they finished their long winter's nap.

Lynn Ball climbed into a bear's den to capture this picture of a cub sleeping with its mother. /Lynn Ball, Ottawa Citizen

Death at the track: Riccardo Paletti was crushed in his car at the 1982 Grand Prix. /Doug Ball, Canadian Press

Death at the Grand Prix

By Doug Ball

There was little joy as we got ready for the annual Canadian Grand Prix in Montreal on June 13, 1982. Shortly before, Canadian racing hero Gilles Villeneuve had died qualifying for the Belgian Grand Prix at Zolder racetrack on May 8.

As usual, *The Canadian Press* set its darkroom up in a building not far from the pit area. We attract a lot of freelance photographers to this event. The deal was that we'd give them accreditation but they'd work for us on Sunday and would be paid *only* if we used a photo.

By race day, we had the whole track covered by freelancers including one in the pit area. I was shooting the start of the race from 200 yards down the track where it starts a slight right turn. This corner was known as a "good photo opportunity".

Just after the start of the race, I would collect rolls of film from a couple of other photogs who shot the start and get it on the wire. The *Associated Press* wanted the pictures ASAP as foreign newspapers were much more interested than North American in Formula One racing.

The start was its normal mass confusion with a lot of tire smoke. But then I saw cars going in different directions and then more smoke than normal. I saw the race had stopped so I got off my stand on the outside of the track, ran across the track and up inside it until I got to more confusion.

They were trying to put out a fire in a racecar that looked like it had hit a wall at great speed. I overheard some say that Italian Riccardo Paletti had smashed his Osella into the back of stalled pole sitter Didier Pironi in his Ferrari. Other drivers managed to avoid Pironi but with all the smoke coming off the racecars' tires and Paletti's back row start, he was blinded, driving straight into Pironi at an estimated 100 mph.

Paletti was crushed into a two or three square foot area. The steering wheel was touching his helmet. At first, his head moved a bit but then it just rested against the wheel. Pironi was helping the safety staff put the fire out.

Doug evaded track security to get photos of the attempted rescue.
Doug Ball, Canadian Press

Security stopped the photographers and reporters in the pits from going to the accident site but they hadn't expected anyone coming up the track. I got wide-angle stuff showing all the things going on. I was so close I was almost leaning over the front right side of the mangled car. I backed up and got some close shots of the trapped driver. I was there long enough to change film in one camera before security gave me the heave-ho.

I picked up the film from the photographer in the pits, who said he couldn't get anything, and headed for the darkroom. I souped the film and called Toronto *CP Pictures*. I moved the first picture but wasn't yet ready to send my second when the editor in Toronto said *AP* was saying go ahead, the *AP* network was open around the world for me to send as many pictures as I chose. It was a satisfying feeling for a photojournalist.

A few days later a great friend and competitor Bob Carroll of *United Press International* sent me an envelope filled with newspaper clippings. Aside from one photo of Paletti's wrecked racecar being hoisted away, the rest were by *The Canadian Press*.

Riccardo Paletti, born June 15, 1958, died June 13, 1982.

Barely There at Surfers' Paradise

By Doug Ball

I lived in Australia in the late '60s during a two-year working trip around the world with my brother, Lynn. So about a year before the 1982 Commonwealth Games in Brisbane, I arranged with my boss Jack Picketts in Toronto to be the photographer for *The Canadian Press* at the XII Games.

In 1969, I had worked in the darkroom at the *Melbourne Herald Sun*, Australia's biggest-selling daily newspaper, and played hockey for the Victoria State Team. I was thrilled to have an opportunity to go back and revisit a wonderful country.

About a week before the Games, Sept. 30 through Oct. 9, I went out everyday looking for feature pictures of Canadian athletes settling into Aussie life. One day, I headed for Surfers' Paradise to see if any athletes were enjoying that famous stretch of sun, sand and rolling breakers. There were only a few Canadian athletes around so I went back the following day. Finally there were a lot of red and white shirts on the beach.

I noticed, right away, that there were a lot of topless girls on the beach also. I looked at them only through my lens, though. Wow, it sure wasn't like Grand Bend or Sauble Beach in 1982.

This was great but *how* was I going to show this to people buying newspapers in Canada? I went over to a group soaking up the sun. There were two guys and a girl and all were topless. Seems fair to me! I introduced myself and asked if I could photograph the girl with some Canadian athletes. Her boyfriend, it turned out, jumped up and said, "No worries, mate! Come on, Melissa."

I rounded up three Canadian badminton players walking down the beach and took a shot of Melissa's back as she walked past the guys. The expression on their faces made the picture.

It was on the front page of *The Toronto Star* the next day.

Doug Ball, Canadian Press

Tiny Tim Tromps the Tulips

By Lynn Ball

The most unlikely thing Tiny Tim could do was tiptoe through the tulips. Tall, gangly, awkward, with his joints oddly hinged, he could tiptoe through the tulips with the dexterity of a bull tiptoeing through a rose garden.

The '60s signature hit of this American novelty performer had been *Tiptoe Through The Tulips*, which was why he was the Ottawa Tulip Festival's celebrity guest in 1983.

The small crowd gathered at the Ottawa airport for his arrival was not disappointed when the frizzy-haired singer with the huge nose and camp falsetto voice clumped through the gate toting his belongings in his trademark shopping bags.

The organizers had a vintage Packard with a rumble seat waiting to give Tiny Tim (Herbert Khaury) a tour of the tulips and show him off while taking him to his hotel. After a struggle, we wrestled the robust 6'1" Tiny into the rumble seat and headed off to look at the tulips. The other photographers had left by then, and I made arrangements with the driver to stop by a tulip bed. We stopped on The Driveway near Fifth Avenue and, again after a struggle with his bony structure, we extracted Tiny from the rumble seat.

Strumming his ukulele, he sang us a few songs including one that he composed about Chuck and Lady Di. I asked him if he would tiptoe through the tulips while he sang his biggest hit. Away he went, strumming and singing through the tulips. I was laughing so hard I could hardly take the pictures. It was hardly a tiptoe. It is still one of my favourite pictures. Tiny Tim (who died in 1996) was such a hit with Ottawans he stayed on, on his own dime, for a few days past his contract to sing at some senior citizens' residences.

Lynn Ball, Ottawa Citizen

To Lynn Ball With Best Wishes (great shot!) Marc Garneau

An incredible noise, a blast of wind: "the most impressive sight I have ever seen." /Lynn Ball, Ottawa Citizen

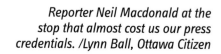

Reporter Neil Macdonald at the stop that almost cost us our press credentials. /Lynn Ball, Ottawa Citizen

Our Man in Space

By Lynn Ball

In December 1983 Canada selected five people for its fledgling astronaut program. Barely into the new year, I was at the press conference announcing that Marc Garneau would be our first man in space.

When NASA set an October date for the eight-day mission, I suggested *The Ottawa Citizen* should send its own photographer to cover this historic event. Managing Editor Nelson Skuce agreed it was worth covering and then asked whom did I suggest we send? I just smiled and he said, "Go ahead."

That's how things were done in the '80s. There was a lot of trust but you had to deliver.

Citizen reporter Neil Macdonald, now with *CBC Television*, was writing the story. We headed to Florida well in advance of the Oct. 5 launch date and rented cars on arrival at Orlando airport. I chose a new Lincoln. Macdonald got himself a shiny red Dodge convertible. We picked up our press accreditation at the Kennedy Space Center, about 45 minutes east of Orlando. We were also given NASA's ground rules: The main one on the list was that the press must keep to the roads when driving between the main gates at Kennedy and the media centre. There was to be NO STOPPING. After getting our accreditation, we checked into rooms at Cocoa Beach.

After a couple of days, Neil decided he wanted a picture of himself with his red convertible and some old rockets on display in the no-stop zone. We drove to the area and got out of the car for a couple of fast shots. Security was onto us like a hen on a June bug. Faced with being kicked out before Garneau blasted off and facing an angry *Citizen* management, we felt lucky to get off with a stern warning.

The big day arrived. In the middle of the night, I watched Garneau, payload specialist, and the rest of the crew on Shuttle Mission 41-G get on a bus to be driven to Challenger. I headed to the media centre to set up my cameras for the launch. The countdown began. It was still dark so I was unsure about what exposure to use. The rocket shone white under the floodlights.

Three, two, one, blast off ... click ... click ... click and it was gone.

Then came the big surprise. The rocket blast hit us with an incredible noise and a force of wind that almost knocked me over. I watched as the flame disappeared into the dawn. It was the most impressive sight I have ever seen.

I headed to the *Associated Press's* darkroom, a trailer, where I had made arrangements to process my film, make a print and transmit it to Ottawa. I was pleased with my picture which made Page One in the final edition.

Later, Garneau, a charming gentleman, signed the wire print for me as a souvenir. In return, I gave him a poster-sized colour print that he hung behind his desk. I described what it was like to experience a rocket blast-off almost six kilometres from the launch site. He said it sounded more exciting from the ground than it was in the space capsule.

Riding Rooster's Raging Bull

By Lynn Ball

After Challenger's liftoff, reporter Neil Macdonald and I left the launch site to fly to the Johnson Space Center in Houston to await the Oct. 13 landing. We needed a car. At a row of quiet car rental booths, Neil shouted out, "Who will give us the best deal on a convertible?"

One lady yelled out, "I'll give you a Lincoln Town Car for $169 a week." "Is that corporate rates?" "This is half your corporate rate." So off we went in an opulent powder blue Lincoln Town Car.

Macdonald had a desire to see Gillies, a bar made famous by the movie *Urban Cowboy*. Gillies was not busy and it was easy to find a parking spot in the large pot-holed, puddle-filled parking lot.

Neil, a big, strapping ex-paratrooper, wanted to take a ride on the mechanical bull. Rooster, the bull's operator, briefed us on technique and Neil climbed on. A small crowd had gathered to watch the tall Canadian cowboy.

The small wiry man with a large Texas drawl asked if Neil was ready. Neil gave him a wave. In no time, you could see that the rider was losing his grip. Then he flew through the air and went down on his right shoulder. Hard.

Then it was my turn. It wasn't easy but it was fun. I managed to stay on.

A small woman asked for a turn. She and her husband were honeymooning in Texas. She stayed on the full time. It was an elegant ride. Not to be shown up, Neil made a comment to Rooster that he'd probably turned up the action much more for his ride.

"Hell, no," said Rooster. "I had the broad turned up three times more than you," he cracked to snickering onlookers.

Lynn's photo hangs on the wall behind astronaut Marc Garneau. /Lynn Ball, Ottawa Citizen

Leonard Cohen on a bench in Montreal; opposite page, Cohen meets writer Chris Cobb; inside, coffee and cigarettes. /Lynn Ball, Ottawa Citizen

Getting to Know Leonard Cohen

By Lynn Ball

When I was assigned on March 29, 1984, to shoot the poet and singer Leonard Cohen at home in Montreal, I had difficulty finding his place because of an error on the assignment sheet. The name of his street was spelled wrong. Finally I found a street that might be the right one. I went to the door and knocked but there was a further complication. I didn't know what Cohen looked like.

"I'm Lynn Ball from *The Ottawa Citizen* and I'm looking for Leonard Cohen," I said to the lean dark-haired man answering the door.

"I'm Leonard Cohen," he said, "Come on in."

Cohen took me into his kitchen and we sat at the table making small talk for quite awhile. We were waiting for *Citizen* reporter Chris Cobb to join us. Cohen then asked me if I would like coffee. While he was filling the pot and spooning coffee, I asked him if I could take a few pictures.

Then we sat, drinking coffee, waiting for Cobb. After coffee we went into his sparsely furnished living room and he played the guitar while I watched and took some more photographs as he composed music.

Then he said he had to go to the store so we got our coats on and headed out. Just outside was a small park where Cohen in his "horsehide" coat posed for some more shots. Then we went shopping.

Hours late, Cobb arrived, embarrassed and apologetic. Some of Cohen's friends came over during the interview and he played his keyboard and sang a little. It was quite a day; one does not often get to spend such private time with a performer of Cohen's stature.

He was in Ottawa a few weeks later and I brought some prints over to the Chateau Laurier. He signed one "for Lynn 'the great eye' many thanks, Leonard Cohen" and told me the pictures were really good.

While waiting for entertainment writer Chris Cobb to show up, Lynn Ball used his time to take pictures of a relaxed and patient Leonard Cohen.
Lynn Ball, Ottawa Citizen

for Lynn
"the great eye"
many thanks
Leonard Cohen

A silhouetted lobster fisherman, Clarence Gauthier, prepares his traps in Prince Edward Island. /Doug Ball

Moonshine Shot Was a Still Photo

By Doug Ball

Sometimes the most memorable shots didn't quite cut it.

On June 6, 1984, I was in Toronto with 99 other photographers from around the world to shoot an edition for *A Day in The Life* books. This book, one of a series on various countries, was to be *A Day in the Life of Canada.*

We were to fan out across the country and precisely at 12:00 a.m. on June 8 begin shooting. Everything we shot that day was fodder for a book that came out Nov. 1, 1985. All of us received airline tickets, some expense money and lots of film. From 100,000 images produced, editor Rick Smolen of Collins Publishers compiled a 221-page coffee-table book of black and white and colour photos with maps and text. The result was a candid presentation of daily life in Canada.

I was allotted a third of Prince Edward Island and a room at the Panmure Island Lighthouse. The day before the shoot I scouted locations for sunrises, sunsets and old general stores as the editor wanted pictures of people opening up their businesses in the morning.

It was a very busy June 8 for me. I didn't stop. Some photographs were planned and others were drive-by shootings. Fishermen with lobster traps, great blue herons wading in the marshes, lighthouses, feeding time for a newborn baby, seals on the beach and a local fellow making moonshine whisky.

The moonshine photo took two days to arrange. I had been going to the island for many years so not being a stranger opened some doors a lot more quickly than it might normally.

It was the last shot of the day. I felt like James Bond making phone calls and talking to certain people at the last minute to complete the job. We drove a truck out into the woods and came upon a shack lit by our headlights. The still's operator didn't want to be in the photo, at first, but I convinced him that his face wouldn't show. He pulled his hat down over his head as I tried to show people how moonshine is made.

I told him that the book would be out in a few months and promised to take a photo that wouldn't give the location away to police.

"No problem. The still is never in one place for too long," he said.

In P.E.I., the boys drink it straight but the girls usually cut it with orange juice.

I thought it tasted a lot like lighter fluid.

(The moonshiner need not have worried. The picture shown here did not make it into A Day In The Life Of Canada.*)*

A masked moonshiner shows off his still. /Doug Ball

Cyan printer Magenta printer Yellow printer

darkest bar is printer color

The Mulroneys bought $4,500 worth of reprints of this victory night picture. /Lynn Ball, Ottawa Citizen

To Victory and Fast Cars

By Lynn Ball

Brian Mulroney was the favourite son in the 1984 federal election. On Sept. 4, he was eagerly awaiting the call in his remote Quebec riding of Baie Comeau and I was assigned to go there for his victory speech.

Don't organize the trip, *Ottawa Citizen* managers said. We'll do it for you. This was a first! Normally I organized my own road trips. The travel itinerary they set up for me went as follows: Fly from Gatineau to Quebec City. Drive by rented car to Baie Comeau. (On the north shore of the St. Lawrence River, the town was a 425-kilometre journey from Quebec City.) Drive back after the speech to Quebec City. Fly to Gatineau with the film so *The Citizen* would have the original negatives for the highest quality reproduction. Gatineau's airport, a small one, is near Ottawa on the Quebec side of the Ottawa River.

I suggested this plan might not work. The Liberals' John Turner was in Vancouver and Mulroney wouldn't speak until Turner had conceded defeat. With the three-hour time difference between British Columbia and Quebec, the Progressive Conservative leader's remarks would be very late.

Brian will be out sooner, they said. Who was kidding whom? I had covered elections since the Diefenbaker days and a victor never spoke before his opponent called it over. There was another hidden snag: The Saguenay River night ferry ran only once an hour.

I didn't find this out until I was on the road from Quebec City to Baie Comeau.

On the day before the election, I flew to Quebec City and at the airport terminal I went to pick up a Chevrolet Caprice I had reserved. The lady didn't have a Caprice but she was certain I would like the car they had ready for me. It was a brand new Camaro Z28. As Chuck Berry would say, now I could really motorvate!

I enjoyed the drive to Baie Comeau. I put the car through its paces and it took it well in stride.

Election day dawned dull and rainy. After I got a shot of the Mulroney couple voting, the rest of the day was easy as I waited for the election results that night. I had an arrangement with *The Canadian Press* to use their dark-room and they would transmit my pictures to *The Citizen*. Also, they would have access to all of my pictures, Ottawa out, of course.

It was a party. Results rolled in and the cheers came ever louder as the seat count passed majority and kept on rising. Finally late in the night after Turner conceded in Vancouver, Brian and Mila

Mulroney with their children appeared on stage and Brian accepted the job of Prime Minister-elect of Canada. A thrilled Baie Comeau celebrated on past the wee hours.

It was far too late to drive back to Quebec City so *CP* developed my film. During the editing process, I pointed out one of Brian and Mila hugging and waving to *CP* photographer Peter Bregg. Bregg really liked it so it was the first picture to move on the *CP* network. That meant *The Citizen* would get its Page One shot right away and wouldn't have to wait until the wire service had moved all of its pictures first.

It was well into the early morning when all of the darkroom work was done. I was able to bum a ride back to Ottawa on Mulroney's plane the next day. I would have to leave the Z28 at the Baie Comeau airport even though I found out later there was a $400 drop-off charge. I gave Bregg a lift to the airport.

There is a long flat straight stretch of highway on the route to the Baie Comeau airport. When we hit this section, I floored it and kept it there the entire length, maybe two miles. I noticed a car behind us and it looked as if it was trying to keep up but couldn't.

We pulled into the crowded parking lot and drove around slowly looking for a parking spot. The car following us pulled in. It was a police car and the cop was looking at us. We pulled into a parking spot and the police car stopped behind us.

"Don't even look at him. Let's just pick up our gear and walk to the prime minister's plane," I said to Bregg.

We got out of the car with our camera gear in hand, walked past the police car and climbed the steps to the plane, no problem at all.

In Baie Comeau that day, the new PM was a powerful force. We flew to Sept-Îles and Mulroney spoke to an entranced crowd. Then back on the plane to Ottawa. On board, Brian was pretty high and went through the plane talking to all.

I had the original victory print that had moved on the wire and the Mulroneys both signed it. They bought $4,500 worth of reprints of that picture from *The Citizen* and handed them out to party faithful across the country to hang in their offices.

Lynn Ball talks with Brian Mulroney on the campaign plane. Ted Grant

Pope John Paul II's meeting with a sick child made front pages. /Lynn Ball, Ottawa Citizen

Travels with Pope John Paul II

By Lynn Ball

Too little sleep, living on coffee, doughnuts and airplane meals, two prime ministers, a Grit to greet the Pope and a Tory to say farewell, constant harassment from security, finding out where you are by looking at your watch, going home by getting on an Air Canada jet – this was the life of a news photographer during Pope John Paul II's 1984 Canadian tour.

The Pope arrived by air in Quebec City on Sept. 9 for a 12-day visit. Stepping off the plane and raising his arm in greeting, he showed off his fancy ox-blood loafers. He walked down the ramp, bent down and kissed the ground. Rising to his feet, he was welcomed by Liberal Prime Minister John Turner and his wife, Geills. John Paul then moved on to a receiving line of about 100 dignitaries.

The host broadcaster, the *Canadian Broadcasting Corporation*, had its camera blocking his face. "*CBC* get out of the way," I started chanting and the other news photographers joined in. "*CBC* get out of the way." We were kept a long way away and had to use 300 and 400 mm lenses most of the tour.

Right away, *CBC* decided to get right in his face so we couldn't see the Pope at all. Our chant, "*CBC* get out of the way!" became so loud, the pontiff actually stopped and looked our way to see what the noise was. We kept it up. It was making great TV so *CBC* backed off and we all got our shots.

Security made us take up our positions an hour before the Pope arrived. So we often had a lot of time to kill just waiting and sometimes nap-ping on the concrete. I had a nice nap on the Quebec City airport runway waiting for the Pope's arrival.

After the airport formalities, John Paul went into the cathedral in Quebec City. I had to get my film back to my newspaper, *The Ottawa Citizen*, as quickly as possible. Expidair, an Air Canada service for fast delivery of small packages, which the pilot actually carried with him on and off the plane, was the fastest and most reliable way to get the film to the paper. The package had to be at the express counter a half-hour before the scheduled takeoff.

Then I went to the outdoor mass. I didn't have any passes for the pool position but I had my general Papal Visit pass so I managed to get in. I walked up to the front at the base of the stage and got a few shots before security had me removed. Then I went up another aisle and got some more shots. I spotted a security officer talking up his sleeve and a few seconds later I was thrown off the grounds.

That was okay by me, I had what I needed. I had checked and the best way to get the film back to Ottawa was by bus. The 8 p.m. bus from Quebec City to Ottawa arrived at 6 a.m. in time for fresh pictures for *The Citizen's* final edition.

Weary Lynn Ball resting on the tarmac. /Boris Spremo　　*John Turner (with wife Geills) was prime minister when the Pope arrived in Canada. /Lynn Ball, Ottawa Citizen*

First Nations people in Ste.-Anne-de-Beaupré reach out to touch the Pope's robe. /Lynn Ball, Ottawa Citizen

At 9 p.m. I was back at my hotel after a 14-hour workday. Early the next morning we were going to the shrine at Ste.-Anne-de-Beaupré. The RCMP handed out pool passes on the train. I didn't get one so I'd be on my own again trying to get in positions to get some good pictures.

Ste.-Anne-de-Beaupré was tough. The visit was an event for First Nations people and they all wanted to touch him, pulling on his robes as he passed. I ended up on a wall beside the stairs into the shrine and had a good view of the Pope. When he spoke from his covered chair I was on the same level and quite close.

I saw the RCMP security guards looking at me but they couldn't move during Papal prayers. When the Pope's entourage had fled the crowd, the RCMP were on me. I told them I was working and could hardly say the RCMP wouldn't allow pictures. I told them I would keep on getting past their security and so would all of the other news photographers assigned to the papal tour.

The next day, the RCMP media liaison officer on the media plane gave us large fluorescent green stickers to put on our press passes. By breaching their security, we were driving the RCMP crazy, he said. These special passes allowed us access to all positions; it made things easier for the RCMP and also for the photographers.

Next stop was Cap-de-la-Madeleine enroute to Montreal but I had to get my film back to *The Citizen*. With written directions and a $50 bill, I found someone willing to take my film to the Quebec City airport and send it by Expidair.

On the train we noticed it was raining and our rain gear, naturally, was in our suitcases, which we didn't have access to. There were some plastic storage bags on the train with VIA on them. These fit nicely on your head and would make a good rain hat.

Boris Spremo, *The Toronto Star's* award-winning photographer and a true character, fashioned a hat by taping the top corners of the white bag and drawing a cross on it with a marking pencil to resemble the Pope's mitre. When the train slowed through towns it was noticed that people thought Spremo was the pontiff.

Pope brings message of faith

An estimated 300,000 attend papal mass at Quebec City's Laval University

300,000 flock to Quebec mass

By Louise Crosby
Citizen staff writer

QUEBEC — Pope John Paul stepped off the plane and into the hearts of Quebeckers Sunday...

Pope John Paul arrives in Quebec Sunday to begin historic tour of Canada

Papal visit
- 'Soft-sell' Pope
- Security passes test
- The changed church
- TV schedule

— pages 33, 34

John Paul captures hearts of Quebeckers

By Aileen McCabe
Southam News

Pope kisses 10-year-old Jasmine Wegrzyka

Ottawa reporter shot at over election stories

By Hugh Adami and Bert Hill

Toughen sentences, parole Ont. justice minister says

KITCHENER, Ont. (CP) —

Someone put a tablecloth around his shoulders. Holding his monopod and wearing his papal-like hat and white robes, Spremo blessed the crowds as the train glided slowly through small towns. The crowds went wild thinking they were being blessed by the Pope.

We were told the Pope was sleeping in a car behind us. Later we heard that *The Star* had not been impressed with Spremo's impersonation.

It was a soggy event at Cap-de-la-Madeleine and when I had enough pictures, I left to find a place to drop off my film. Pat McGrath, fellow *Citizen* photographer, was already on his way out from Ottawa to pick it up. I called in to give the location of the gas bar. McGrath would make regular calls back to the newspaper until he found out where it was; pick it up and race back to the paper. This was in the days before cell phones.

Citizen photo editor Richard Starnes said the Ste.-Anne-de-Beaupré pictures, which I'd taken earlier, were "fantastic," when I called in to give him the gas bar's location to pass on to McGrath.

So it was working, the Pope's itinerary in one hand and an Air Canada flight schedule in the other.

Youth rally at Olympic Stadium; stick to straight and narrow, pope advises

Pontiff came to Quebec as pastor, not prophet

Pope preached gentleness and compassion in Olympic Stadium homily

Another long day, 8 a.m. to midnight, was over and we were now in Montreal where there was a 6 a.m. media briefing. I sent the rolls of film from the morning visit to St. Joseph's Oratory to Ottawa by bus and later handed the film from the Big O's happening to McGrath to be driven the two-and-a-half hours to the newspaper. It had been a 14-hour day.

The next morning, we flew from Montreal to St. John's, Nfld., where at a service at Flatrock, John Paul blessed the fishing boats anchored at sea in the shape of a cross. Film was Expidaired back to Ottawa at 4 p.m.

That evening, a youth rally was held in rain driving sideways followed by a trip to the airport to send film. It had been a 19-hour day this time and I was starving. Everything was closed. I ran into *Southam News* reporter Peter Calamai in the hotel lobby and he gave me a bag of gorp (raisins and peanuts). Early the next morning after the usual coffee and doughnuts breakfast, we flew to Moncton, N.B.

After mass, I gave my film and $30 to Peter Jones, a young and ambitious Moncton photographer, who ran it to the airport for shipping to Ottawa while I flew on to Halifax.

That evening, I made up for missing meals at the Five Fishermen restaurant in Halifax. Ted Church, a news photographer with *The Montreal Gazette*, says I ate half of the items on the menu.

At Halifax's Izaak Walton Killam Hospital for seriously ill children, as the Pope was walking through and blessing the youngsters, a *Toronto Sun* photographer was knocked off the ladder he was carrying around to see over the crowd. He and the ladder made a loud clatter as they hit the floor. Hearing this, John Paul paused from blessing the children and looked to see if the photographer was all right.

The film was shipped to Ottawa and the entourage flew to Toronto, where the Pope's arrival and appointments were duly recorded and reported and a helpful cab driver took the film to the airport.

At 10 p.m., Ted Church and I got a bus to Midland arriving at 1 a.m. to find the only place to sleep was the gym floor of the YMCA. While trying to find the Y, we became lost in the woods of a large park. Finally we found the Y and were given sleeping bags and bedded down on some foam tumbling mats.

The Toronto Star's Boris Spremo as the Pope. /Lynn Ball, Ottawa Citizen

It was now very late and I fell asleep at once, waking suddenly when I heard some stirring next to me. There had been a vacant spot beside mine, now it was being occupied. As I opened my eyes a pair of pants was being dropped and a woman's butt was almost in my face as she crawled into her sleeping bag. I was in a deep sleep just before this interruption and thought I was in some sort of weird dream. I went back to sleep and was up early to wash my face and brush my teeth in the gym's facilities.

After the service at the Martyrs' Shrine we left for Toronto and at 6 a.m. the next morning we were on a plane to Winnipeg. Now the hard times for shipping film would start.

In the east, the time difference was to my advantage, but in the west each time zone took an hour off the deadline time.

In Winnipeg, John Paul visited St. Vladimir and Olga Ukrainian Cathedral. We got some beautiful shots of the Pontiff blessing the women in colourful traditional dresses. Now I had to get my film to the airport. I walked down the street calling out, "Can anyone drive me to the airport?"

I did this several times before a young fellow came up and said his car was only a couple of blocks away and he would drive me. His 400 Pontiac Firebird was a fast car and we took off for the airport, as I didn't have much time.

We came to a red light and he stopped even though there were no cars coming. "Go on through. All the cops are with the Pope." On we went running red lights all the way to the airport. My driver, Norbert Iwan, a recent Polish immigrant, liked fast American cars and appreciated the $30 I gave him for the ride.

The film just made it onto the next flight to Ottawa. I even had a few minutes to visit with Aunt Eileen and cousin Jeff before we flew on to Edmonton.

I was up at 4:30 a.m. for the usual lobby breakfast of doughnuts and coffee and on a bus an hour later to ride out to the mass north of the city. Edmonton's airport is south of the city and the mass site was secured, no traffic in or out. I found an empty bus headed back into town and bummed a ride urging the driver to go faster.

He dropped me on a deserted downtown street. I thought I'd never find a cab but luck was with me. I spotted a baffed-out Plymouth Volare for hire and told the driver to go as fast as possible. He did. I thought the car was going to come apart, vibrating and shaking all the way to the airport.

At the Air Canada express counter, the attendant told me it was too late to make Expidair as the flight was taking off in a few minutes. I put a crisp $50 bill on the counter. "Don't worry. This package will make it," he smiled, turning and running through the terminal to hand it to the pilot personally.

After a leisurely drive back to Edmonton, I ran into Ted Church and a couple of other news photographers and we went out for supper at a Greek restaurant. We needed a good meal as the next day was from Hell, even if we were with the Pope. During the flight to Fort Simpson, N.W.T., François Paulette, who was from Fort Simpson, expressed some concerns about landing. The settlement, on the banks of the Mackenzie River 500 kilometres south of the Arctic Circle, was usually engulfed in fog at this time of year.

Sure enough it was. Our media plane and the plane carrying the Pope circled around above socked-in Fort Simpson as we prayed for the fog to clear, but it didn't. We circled until we were low on fuel and then it was announced that we'd land in Yellowknife to refuel and fly on to Vancouver. The Pope's plane had enough fuel. It would fly direct to Vancouver.

Seconds after takeoff from Yellowknife our plane banked hard and it was announced that we would be landing again as the Pope had changed his mind and would soon land to meet some natives in Yellowknife.

We landed but were not allowed to deplane until a plane filled with RCMP officers arrived to guard the Pope from us. For no apparent reason the RCMP started pushing us around as we walked to the terminal. We couldn't figure what was going on. We were outnumbered.

In the tiny airport, we were told John Paul would meet and bless some Native people. The photographers were penned at one end and a line of local residents was started in front of us and stretched away to the other side of the terminal where the Pope was addressing the crowd through a megaphone.

A shout of "Santo Padre, Santo Padre, el Papa" from Lynn got the Pope's attention. /Lynn Ball, Ottawa Citizen

Media souvenirs of the papal tour.

I was standing on a chair against the wall. Ted Church was beside me. The Pope appeared and walked in front of us shaking hands and blessing the faithful as he worked his way along the line.

Sounds great except for one thing. All we could see was the Papal back. The fourth person in line was wearing a full-length moosehide coat decorated with colourful beadwork. This man took off his coat and gave it to the Pope. John Paul started to put the coat on with his back to us.

At that time, the Pope had several Vatican photographers with him who took pictures of everyone he met to send back to the parishes, so a Vatican official told me. When one of these photos was about to be taken, these photographers would say something to John Paul and he would look up and smile and sometimes give the little papal finger wave.

I'd heard them say it and I learned how to say it too. I nudged Ted Church.

"Listen to this."

With my camera focused on John Paul's back, I called, "Santo Padre, Santo Padre, el Papa."

With that, the Pope wheeled instantly about and gave me the papal wave and I snapped pictures.

WOW, I had spoken to the Pope and he had acknowledged it.

The RCMP herded us back across the runway and onto the plane and we flew to Vancouver. Tight security meant circling until the Pope's plane was down. That meant missing the Vancouver event.

I headed for *The Canadian Press* office in Vancouver to develop my film and move it on the wire to *The Citizen*. With the three-hour time difference, wire photo was the only way to get the pictures to Ottawa to make dead-line.

The news co-operative wanted the Yellowknife pictures as well. As we left Yellowknife right after the airport event no wire pictures had moved from there but *CP* had heard the story and was keen to see my pictures.

The pictures proved out. I had the Pope in his fancy moosehide coat looking right into my lens, giving me the wave. Nobody else got the shot. It moved full network and got play all across the country.

The Ottawa Citizen used it on the front of the papal visit special section and the nation's capital French newspaper *Le Droit* ran it on its front page.

Early the next morning the media gathered on the runway at the Van-couver airport to board the 727. Boris Spremo, quite subdued since playing the Pope on the train to Montreal earlier, said to me, "Lynn, take picture of Boris with Pope hat."

We walked away from the plane and Boris put on his, by then infa-mous, hat for a couple of quick pictures, then stashed it back in his camera bag. We flew east to Ottawa, last stop on the tour.

The Pope was met by a new prime minister, Brian Mulroney. The Conservatives had been elected on Sept. 4 but Mulroney had not officially taken office when the Pope arrived in Quebec City on Sept. 9.

I couldn't get shots of John Paul arriving in the capital but I managed to get into the crowd once I got off the runway. I was behind a fence and a row of people standing on chairs so they could see over the fence and the rows of heads for a view of the Pope.

Norbert Iwan and his fast Firebird delivered Lynn and his film to the airport. Lynn Ball, Ottawa Citizen

Brian Mulroney (with wife Mila) was prime minister when the Pope departed Canada. /Lynn Ball, Ottawa Citizen

I was trying to squeeze through the mass of people when an RCMP officer on the papal tour recognized my situation and me. He went up to one person standing on a chair and said the chair was reserved and to get down.

I hopped up just as Mulroney and his wife, Mila, welcomed the Pope to Ottawa. The scene was backlit by the afternoon sun and I could hardly see them, let alone focus through the sun flare in the lens. I was on my tiptoes using a 300 mm lens. I took a few frames and to my surprise, they turned out very well.

The next day there was the big papal show in the capital and that evening the Pope left Canada.

What a trip! I think we were the only newspaper in the country to have fresh original pictures of the papal tour every day. Other papers used wire-photos. Some, with photographers assigned to the tour, later put out a book on the papal visit for their readers.

It was a tough go but I really enjoyed the challenge. Air Canada never missed and all of the film made it back to Ottawa on schedule.

The Pilgrim Pope travelled the world to more places and spoke to more people than any other Pontiff in the history of the Roman Catholic Church. In his 26 years at the Vatican, John Paul II visited almost 130 countries. He was in Canada three times, returning to spend five hours in Fort Simpson in 1987 and in 2002, ailing and frail, he thrilled thousands at World Youth Day in Toronto. He died April 2, 2005 at age 84.

Bobby's Performance above Par

By Doug Ball

I've missed only two British Open Championships since 1983 when American Tom Watson won his last title of five at Royal Birkdale, now swanky Southport, not far from Blackpool.

In 1985, I took along my buddy Ted Cullen from Montreal's Whitlock Golf and Curling Club to the 1985 Open at Royal St. George's Golf Club in Sandwich, near Dover. Peter Bregg, a former staffer for *The Canadian Press*, (who made the best decision of his life when he asked me to be the best man at his marriage to Diane) was running the Open's photo set-up for *The Associated Press*.

I wasn't working for any news outlet specifically but I managed to obtain a photo pass anyway. Only those photographers with passes can carry cameras on the golf course during the four days of the Open Championship.

One day, I'm near the 18th hole where Peter Jacobsen is waiting to putt. Suddenly a male streaker darts out of the crowd and skips across the green. As he passes Jacobsen, the American hits him with a perfect football tackle and nails his naked body to the ground. When the police take over, Jacobsen jumps to his feet and performs an end zone celebration dance for his great tackle.

I get a few frames of the Jacobsen tackle and his celebratory performance but the best picture is yet to come. Two bobbies, as police are called in England, walk the streaker off the green, each holding the man by an arm, in full frontal view of the crowd in the stands.

One of the bobbies removes his helmet and holds it over the streaker's privates as the threesome walks past the stands to thunderous applause.

Sandy Lyle of Britain won the 1985 British Open Championship.

That's not usually where you hang your hat, except at the British Open. /Doug Ball

Mainland Dandies Cover a Newfoundland Air Crash

By Lynn Ball

On Dec. 12, 1985, on my way into work at *The Ottawa Citizen* I heard on the car radio that an Arrow Airlines DC-8 had crashed and burned seconds after takeoff from Gander, Nfld., killing all 248 passengers and crew of eight.

Flight 1285 was a charter carrying U.S. soldiers home from the Middle East in time for Christmas and had stopped in Gander for refuelling. Most were members of the 101st Airborne Division (Air Assault). They were returning to base station Fort Campbell, Ky., after completing a six-month tour of duty in the Sinai with Multinational Force and Observers, a peacekeeping mission.

That morning I was assigned to cover the Gander tragedy with *Citizen* reporter Neil Macdonald. The only flight we could get was to Halifax and then on to St. John's where we rented a car to drive the 331 kilometres to Gander.

It was dark and snowing heavily by the time we headed for the crash site in a Chevy Caprice. Neil was driving and we hadn't gone far before we were pulled over by the RCMP for speeding. The police officer asked Neil for his driver's licence.

"It's in my purse," Neil said, and turning to me he said, "Would you get my purse? It's in the back seat." I leaned back, picked it up and handed it to him. Neil took out his licence and I sat there with a big grin on my face. The cop returned to his vehicle.

"What's so funny?"

"Every cop on the radio in Newfoundland now knows that he's stopped a couple of mainland dandies carrying purses," I replied. "Neil, men don't carry purses in Newfoundland."

Image-conscious Neil said, "Oh shit." He hopped out of the car without a coat and stood by the police cruiser in the blowing snow, kicking the snow and doing other macho things until the officer had the ticket written.

A frozen Neil got back in the car with the $25 speeding ticket and told me the cop said he'd stopped us because the chances of hitting a moose in a snowstorm while speeding were rather high.

Farther up the road in Terra Nova National Park while I was driving we did see Bullwinkle, giant antlers and all, standing on the highway in the other lane. He just stood there and watched us as we drove by.

In Gander we checked out the airport and were told to come back early in the morning. Very tired, we got a hotel room. After an early breakfast, we headed back to the airport for the media briefings. Information was sketchy and they wouldn't allow photographers near the crash site.

Some negotiations with officials resulted in one photographer being allowed to shoot pictures from a helicopter over the crash site. None of the wire services trusted each other not to withhold a good shot so I was given the honour of pool photog with my pictures offered to all in the media.

It was getting late in the day when we were told the helicopter was cancelled and we would all be going to the site by military bus. There was a small road through the crash area and we would drive through it and turn around to go through again and back to Gander airport.

The sun was right on the horizon when we drove through the wreckage. I saw an engine and a couple of other small pieces that looked like they had come from an airplane but there wasn't much left.

Since the plane had just refuelled it burned up completely on crashing. Total devastation. A very sad sight. I used my *Canadian Press* darkroom to develop and transmit two pictures back to *The Citizen*.

The area of the crash, four kilometres east of the town of Gander, is now Peacekeeper Park. A Silent Witness Memorial stands in memory of the soldiers and crew.

The site of the Gander aircrash is now Peacekeeper Park. /Lynn Ball, Ottawa Citizen

"My favourite picture was the shot of Sarah waving at me out the carriage window." /Lynn Ball, Ottawa Citizen

How to Photograph a Royal Wedding

By Lynn Ball

Shooting Charles and Diana's wedding had given me some insight into what was required in photographing royal nuptials. This time Prince Andrew was to wed Lady Sarah Ferguson on July 23, 1986.

First on the agenda was phoning Buckingham Palace for press accreditation and to reserve a location outside Westminster Abbey. I also booked flights to London and back, rented a car and arranged for a room at the Westbury Hotel.

But there was another critical element. I arranged with cabbie Danny Doyle to meet me across Westminster Bridge after the wedding to drive me quickly to the airport. The timing was going to be tight.

I was allotted a position on a row of risers built across the street from Westminster Abbey. It was a two-tier affair at least 100 yards long and with three feet for each photog there would be a lot of us. I went down to check the structure the night before the wedding. I walked up and down both levels checking out the angles. I preferred the upper level and not right in front of the Abbey. I needed many different pictures and various positions on the risers didn't allow it. Some positions put a hydro pole in the background.

Finally I picked a spot but it was already taken. Tripods were taped to the railing with the photographer's business card in place with the space wanted taped off. These were all larger than the three feet we were allowed. I gently removed the tape and moved it along so that all the spots were three feet wide. I did this to three spots left and right of the space I wanted, then wrote "3 feet only" on the rail in black marker. I taped my card and tripod in the spot I had created then went back to the Westbury to get some sleep.

The next morning, no one said a word or even noticed what I had done. From this position, the royal carriage would pass in front of me. After the wedding they would come straight towards me before turning away. I would be able to get a shot of the couple in their carriage with a wide-angle lens showing them and Westminster Abbey. Happy, I settled down and planned the shots and got the lenses ready.

Shortly before the ceremony was to start two dogs came along becoming amorous as they got close to the church. Their fun didn't last long as they were picked up and thrown in a van and driven away. The VIP guests and Royals arrived and then the wedding party.

Sarah seemed to be waving right to me through the carriage window as she rode past with her father beside her. I panned the shot using a 300 mm lens on a Nikon 3F camera. With the pomp and ceremony that only the British can pull off, all of the guests were soon inside the Abbey including Canada's Governor General Jeanne Sauvé and her husband, Maurice.

To loud cheers, the newlyweds emerged from the Abbey and walked to a waiting carriage. Sarah, left, and Andrew, on the right, waving to the crowd blocked Andrew's face with their hands. I was using a 400 mm f2.8 lens with a 2X converter making it 800 mm f5.6 for poster quality pictures. The royal couple filled the frame. It was a tight squeeze. The tripod was attached to the tripod mount on the lens and all adjustments were loose so I could move the camera both horizontally and vertically.

I was gambling on the long lens to get a tighter shot that wouldn't have to be blown up much for a full page in *The Ottawa Citizen*, a broadsheet paper. They were on the shady side of the Abbey and at 800 asa I had to shoot at 250th of a second at 5.6, an aperture that was wide open. I had to be very, very careful not to get camera shake, as an 800 mm lens is difficult to hold still especially when loosely mounted on a tripod.

All of a sudden they stopped waving. Smiling, they turned slightly towards me. I got off one shot. There were no more opportunities. Then they got into the carriage and they trotted towards me. It made a wonderful picture. Queen Elizabeth and Sarah's father left together and soon it was all over.

Danny Doyle was waiting for me at the bridge and my brother Doug had film for me to drop off for *The Canadian Press* in Toronto. Danny took our picture and

The Queen Mother and Princess Margaret. /Lynn Ball, Ottawa Citizen

Queen Elizabeth and the Duke of Edinburgh riding out to marry off another prince. /Lynn Ball, Ottawa Citizen

Prince Andrew and Sarah Ferguson. /Lynn Ball, Ottawa Citizen

Prince Andrew and Sarah Ferguson wave to the crowds. /Lynn Ball, Ottawa Citizen

Now, now, none of that. Amorous pooches are swept up by police and carted away in a paddy wagon. /Lynn Ball, Ottawa Citizen

then I hopped into the cab and we made a mad dash to Heathrow. It was close. The flight had been called and was loading when I got there.

Off to Toronto then on to Ottawa, I was in time to develop the film for the next day's editions. The full-size shot of the royal couple smiling outside the Abbey was the full-page cover of the royal wedding souvenir edition.

My favourite picture was the shot of Sarah waving at me out the carriage window. I loved shooting this type of assignment.

What We'd Do for a Picture

By Lynn Ball

In a memorable incident that illustrates the lengths that my subjects and I will sometimes go to please, I was assigned to fly with the SkyHawks in an old C-47 better known as a DC-3. My editor briefed me on the kinds of pictures he wanted of the Canadian Forces parachute team.

He wanted pictures of the eight parachutists holding hands in a circle and other shots of them on their way to the ground. What he didn't realize is that the plane dropped the skydivers off at a cruising speed of 320 kph (200 mph). As they jumped they were gone in a blink, out of sight of anybody on board.

It was a hot, humid day in September 1987 and the air was unstable as we circled above Ottawa. The pilot tried different altitudes between 10,000 and 12,000 feet looking for stable air. It was a very bumpy flight.

The door of the plane was open and exhaust fumes wafted through the cabin. The turbulence and smell of spent fuel was taking its toll on my stomach. I didn't barf but it was close.

When it was time to jump, out they tumbled one by one. I looked out the door after each parachutist left but never saw anything.

Cpl. Paul Burke, who would be the last man to jump, saw I wasn't getting any pictures.

"Get ready," the 22-year-old said, "I'll make sure you get a picture."

He backed up to the door and jumped out backwards, arms raised. I was ready and got a shot and then looked out the door of the plane again and of course saw nothing.

We headed back to Uplands Airport and there wasn't a happier person than me when the wheels touched the runway.

Then I noticed the pilot and ground staff talking about the jump. It seems there was some sort of accident but they didn't tell me what it was.

Later, I found out that when Cpl. Burke hammed his jump for me the wind caught him and held him up. The plane's tail clipped him on the back of his helmet. Unconscious, he plummeted towards downtown Ottawa.

An altitude-sensing device set off by a change in barometric pressure opened his reserve chute seconds before he landed, narrowly missing some trees and a statue, on the lawn of the Supreme Court Building.

Citizen photographer Bruno Schlumberger was at regional headquarters to photograph the SkyHawks' landings. When he saw a parachute not opening on the last man out of the plane he took off at a run and ran all the way to the Supreme Court, about a mile.

He photographed the injured parachutist being attended and transported to hospital by ambulance.

Happily Cpl. Burke did not suffer serious injuries.

Thank you Cpl. Burke.

Cpl. Paul Burke a split second before he was clipped on the head by the aircraft's tail. /Lynn Ball, Ottawa Citizen

Adam Sat Out the Moment

By Lynn Ball

Things were rocking in my hometown, London, on the night of Sept. 10, 1987. It was evident early on as the results came in that a majority was underway for Ontario's Liberal leader David Peterson.

Peterson organizers had a scaffold set up at Centennial Hall for news photographers so they would have a clear view of the leader and his family on stage for the victory speech.

It wasn't for me. I didn't like to be trapped in one spot if there was an opportunity to roam.

With 95 of 130 seats won, the Liberal faithful were anxious for their leader to speak. I went outside and waited by the back door, the most logical entrance for the premier to use.

Sure enough, Peterson and his family came in that way, heading for the stage with me in tow. I stood to one side so I wouldn't block the television cameras and the other photogs, moving in front for a quick shot when the moment was right.

A jubilant premier spoke to supporters, standing with his wife, Shelley, and children, Ben and Chloe, at their sides. The Petersons have three children. Where was Adam?

I moved to get a shot of them before the crowd and there was Adam, hidden behind his mother's skirt, chin propped by a chubby fist, clearly bored. I took a few shots of this comical scene.

The triumphant Petersons waving to the crowd ran on Page One of *The Ottawa Citizen*. Inside was my picture of Adam.

The back exit to Centennial Hall was near the darkroom set up by *The Canadian Press*. On his way out Peterson spotted me and I invited him to come in and see the pictures that had moved on the wire. The photos and the speed in which they were done impressed him.

The next morning, proud and happy, he held court at a breakfast for the media. Things were different at the next election. Defeated on Sept. 6, 1990, by the NDP, a subdued Peterson, who had lost his own seat, left quickly after his short speech. There was no breakfast for us in the morning.

Dad's a winner but some guys just hate politics.
Lynn Ball, Ottawa Citizen

Chance and good timing caught Lévesque's widow appropriately framed. /Lynn Ball, Ottawa Citizen

Sometimes it Pays to Duck

By Lynn Ball

Lynn caught a few shots in the Basilica before he was thrown out.
Lynn Ball, Ottawa Citizen

The streets were jammed with mourners for René Lévesque the day of his funeral. The former Quebec premier and founder of the Parti Québécois died Nov. 1, 1987, at the age of 65. The ceremony began at the Legislature where his body had lain in state and then the casket was driven slowly through the old city to the Basilica. The square outside the Basilica was filled with people of all ages.

The police herded the photographers into a small reserved area across the street from the Basilica's main doors. I didn't like to be penned up with the other photogs because it restricted my chances of getting something different. I floated around and the police kept telling me to move on, so I kept changing location.

I saw Daniel Drolet, reporter for *The Ottawa Citizen*, come out a side door of the Basilica. He was leaving because the press could see "nothing" from the corner where they had to stand. He gave me his pass. There was a pool position for one photographer in the church but it was in the balcony to one side, not the best spot for pictures.

Equipped with Danny's pass, I slipped in the side door and quickly assessed the light. I set my Nikon F3, fitted with a 300 mm lens, to 1/60 of a second at 2.8, giving me a very narrow depth of field. I walked over to the centre aisle at the back of the Basilica. There was the casket surrounded by priests. I started shooting. While focusing, I could see the security people coming for me. I got three frames off before they grabbed me and dragged me back to the side door and physically threw me out.

"Wow!" I hoped the shot would be OK as it is hard to hold a 300 mm lens still at 1/60 of a second. Now I had to get a shot of the casket and mourners leaving the Basilica. I went around to the front. I was inside the barricade and in front of the news photographers' pen and they let me know it. I squatted down because I didn't want to be in their way.

The casket was just emerging from the doors to be carried down the stairs. I couldn't believe my eyes. For a very few seconds, the grieving widow was framed by the casket above her head and the pallbearers on either side. I took a few frames. I had what I needed and I knew it. I took a few shots of the mourners then I had to get back to Ottawa, fast.

It was near dark. On the highway to Montreal, I saw flashing lights in the rearview mirror. As I slowed to the speed limit, a motorcade of Quebec government cars roared by. I figured it was Premier Robert Bourassa's entourage so I got in behind and used them like a rabbit to lead me to Montreal. I made the drive from Quebec City to Ottawa in well under four hours, some of it in a small blizzard.

The next morning, the photograph of Corinne Côté at her husband's funeral was on Page One in *The Ottawa Citizen*. Three colour shots were used inside: the one I snapped of the casket before I was thrown out of the

Basilica, a young tearful girl holding a small Quebec flag and a picture of Lévesque's fellow politicians. *Citizen* publisher Russell Mills liked the Page One picture so much that he enlarged it by a full column for the final edition. After a hard day's work, it was very satisfying.

A face in the crowd at Lévesque's funeral.
Lynn Ball,
Ottawa Citizen

Canada, the snowbound land. Calgary '88 Olympics. /Lynn Ball, Ottawa Citizen

Winner of the Photographers' Downhill Tumbling Race

By Lynn Ball

There are two rules about photographing Olympic skiing events at the top of the mountain: Be a good skier, and let someone else carry your gear.

During the 1988 Calgary Winter Olympics I was loaned to *The Canadian Press* as part of the national pool of about 20 of the best Canadian news photographers. *CP* sent me to Kananaskis for the first week of the Games to cover skiing. The photo crew was lodged near the ski venue at the Rafter 6 Ranch in the foothills of the Rockies. I don't know what we did to merit such mediocre facilities.

I'm a Nikon man but Canon was the official camera of the Olympics. Canon was giving away very attractive bright red Canon Official Camera of the Calgary Olympic Games coats, and I like to collect souvenirs. Ian MacAlpine, a Kingston photographer, gave me a Canon camera to take to the service department to be serviced so I could get a coat. The technician asked me to take the film out of the camera and I didn't know how! Like I said, I'm a Nikon man. But no questions were asked and I got a beautiful official coat.

Our Olympic passes doubled as ski lift tickets. I took advantage of this and spent a couple of days skiing before the Games began. I also used this time to check out a safe slow route down the mountain.

I was assigned to the top of the mountain where the skiers would be going the fastest. If a fall happened, this was where it would occur. I needed an easy path down the mountain, as I am not a very good skier.

We shot some practice runs just to get a feel for things. Finally the big day came and the Olympics were officially open. The men's downhill was the first event – the fastest and most daring event on the slopes.

With skis on and loaded down with camera gear, I took the chairlift to the top of the mountain. Wind could be a problem on Mount Allen and it was windy. Gusts were seen coming as a wall of snow. The men's downhill race was cancelled and it was reported that gusts were clocked between 160 and 210 kilometres an hour.

Blowing snow covered everything and everyone. When I left the photo position at the top of Mount Allen, there was an *Agence France-Presse* photographer from Paris, France, who had lain down and was nearly covered with snow. He said he wasn't leaving until the wind and snow stopped.

I don't know how long he stayed there but I didn't hear of any bodies being found, so I guess he did find his way down.

I packed up my gear and headed back down the mountain. I had to ski across the downhill racecourse before turning down my chosen easy route. Crossing the course, I looked up at the peak. Another blast of wind and snow hit and a Canadian flag fluttered frantically. What a shot! I took off my skis and walked up to the flag and got a couple of shots of the flag in the blowing snow with the sun right behind it.

Back on my skis, I started down the mountain to the *CP* darkroom. Not used to skiing with so much camera gear, I fell many times. My Nikon cameras and lenses spent the night under towels with hair driers blowing to dry them out.

The flag in the snow picture was well received. It looked like a scene from the North Pole. *The Calgary Herald* and *The Ottawa Citizen* used it big on Page One the next day. It was used all around the world including by *USA Today* and *Time Magazine*.

I was off to a good start.

The next morning I had a sore knee from falling so many times while coming down the mountain the day before. One of the film runners was assigned to carry my gear. It turned out that he was third in the Canadian junior men's downhill, so he could ski.

We went up the mountain and I shot the men's downhill event. The start was nearly a vertical drop then a turn with a big net to catch anyone who went off the course. I couldn't believe the speed. Several skiers flew into the net making good pictures, but none of the favourites crashed.

At the end of the event, I gave my cameras to the kid and he flashed off down the hill. I kept one unmotorized Nikon F with a 35 mm lens because there were some VIPs on the hill and if I saw any I was expected to photograph them.

The camera had a long strap and I put it over my head with an arm through the strap so the camera was resting on my back.

I started my charge down Mount Allen on the safe route that I had scouted out. I could ski straight but had trouble turning. I didn't mind the speed. I was enjoying myself ripping down the hill thinking all this fun and I'm getting paid for it.

Suddenly things changed. My safe route down the hill was blocked. They were making a slalom path on my run, I think. Now I had to go down a new part of the mountain and it was steep. I was reaching speeds unknown to me and flying blind over the brows of hills.

At high speed, I went over a hill and below were moguls. Big panic. I tried to turn but I was going so fast I was launched right out of my skis. Flying through the air I started to tumble. I came down on my back right on top of my camera. Everything went black and I saw stars.

When I came to, I was gasping for air as I had had the wind knocked out of me. There was a crowd gathered asking if I was all right. I got on my hands and knees and finally got enough breath to talk. I seemed okay.

"I think I'm all right," I said, as I got to my feet.

Someone retrieved my skis from up the hill and gave them to me. I walked gingerly over to the edge of the moguls, put on my skis and slowly worked my way down the hill.

I wasn't okay. I had cracked some ribs and it was painful. When I was finished work I went to Banff to lay in the hot springs. In fact, I went to the hot springs in Banff every single night while I was at Mount Allen and lived on 292s for the rest of the Games. If I laughed, coughed or sneezed it felt like a knife in my ribs. It was difficult to sleep because every time I moved I awakened in pain.

The next day, the runner had to carry my cameras up and down the mountain and he stayed with me just in case I needed a camera. My ribs were too sore for me to carry anything.

Eventually the pain went away and I still have my prize photo. The Canadian flag in the snow shot won second in the Best Picture from the Games contest. I still have my memories of seeing Elizabeth Manley and Brian Orser win silver medals in figure skating, and hearing the crowd chant "Ralph, Ralph, Ralph" at the closing ceremonies in tribute to Ralph Klein, then mayor of Calgary, for bringing the Olympics to the city.

It was worth my tumble down the mountain.

Evading the Tightest Security Ever!

By Lynn Ball

Security surrounding the president of the United States causes problems for those in the news business. George Bush's 1989 visit to Ottawa was no exception, when we were told security would be "the toughest yet".

Sometimes the best way to beat security is to just do your job.

Air Force One was scheduled to touch down Feb. 11 at 10:45 a.m. *The Ottawa Citizen's* final edition deadline was noon or shortly after. It looked as if it would be impossible for the newspaper to carry a photograph of the president's arrival.

We were told that the only way photographers would be admitted to Hangar 11 at the Canadian Forces Uplands Air Base was to take a secured bus from the National Press Building at 150 Wellington St. in downtown Ottawa. By the time *Citizen* photographer John Major, who was on the bus, could get back to the Baxter Road newsroom in Ottawa's west end, it would be too late for that day's paper.

We were told that the base was under a security blanket. No one was allowed on the base before the president arrived or off the base until the president's motorcade left. No media was allowed except on the special bus.

What a challenge! I had to make the effort to get into Hangar 11, a huge steel-sided building where world leaders visiting the nation's capital deplaned. I drove out Hunt Club Road to Bowesville Road and turned into Uplands Air Base. At the guardhouse I stopped and showed my press accreditation and was waved through. I thought, wow, I just got someone in trouble, and drove on to Hangar 11.

The place was crawling with police in dark suits. Royal Canadian Mounted Police and American Secret Service agents were guarding the hangar's entrance. I just stood by my bright yellow *Citizen* car and loaded my cameras. I picked up my gear and smiled, nodded and kept on walking.

I couldn't believe where I was. I had just walked past all the security that we were told would be the tightest ever. I saw that the media bus had arrived and headed over to catch the last of the briefing. We were led out onto the runway and the presidential jet landed.

I got a nice shot of Prime Minister Brian Mulroney greeting President Bush with an RCMP officer in his red dress uniform looking on. They were getting into their cars. I ran and hopped into mine and zipped out in front of the motorcade, beating them off the base. I continued at high speed to *The Citizen* where I developed the film and printed the picture. The picture was on the page about 50 minutes after the president's plane had touched down.

The photo was Page One for the home-delivered evening editions. *Citizen* readers saw the president's arrival the day of and not the day after, despite "the toughest security yet."

Lynn got around the "toughest security yet" to photograph U.S. President George Bush at Ottawa airport. /Lynn Ball, Ottawa Citizen

Lighting up Bo Diddley

By Lynn Ball

My brother Doug called in the spring of 1991 to say my rock and roll hero Bo Diddley was playing at a car show in Montreal and invited me to come down to see him. With my camera and a bag full of old Bo Diddley LPs I headed off.

We found the stage at the car show and spotted a fellow that looked like a musician.

"Is Bo Diddley here?"

"Yes," he said, and took us to a door behind the stage. He opened it and there was a dejected-looking Bo Diddley in a butterscotch leisure suit with bell-bottomed trousers slumped at the far end of a long narrow room.

"Here are a couple of fans that would like to meet you."

Bo Diddley gave us an unenthusiastic nod.

I walked down the room and pulled out my old Bo Diddley LPs from the 1950s and '60s.

"Would you autograph these?"

His eyes lit up and he looked at me, "Are those yours?"

"I bought them when they were first released," I said.

His mood changed instantly. He was really excited to see his old LPs.

Doug was snapping pictures of us. Bo Diddley hammed it up. He challenged me to arm wrestle and then pretended to draw a pistol on me, a big grin on his face. One of his hits was a song called *Gunslinger* and a line is "... *Now, Bo Diddley didn't stand no mess, he wore a gun on his hip and a rose on his chest.*"

We had a great time with him. He gave me his address to send him some pictures and I got some back from him autographed.

His performance that day was phenomenal. A true legend, he did all of his hits including *Road Runner, Who Do You Love* and many more.

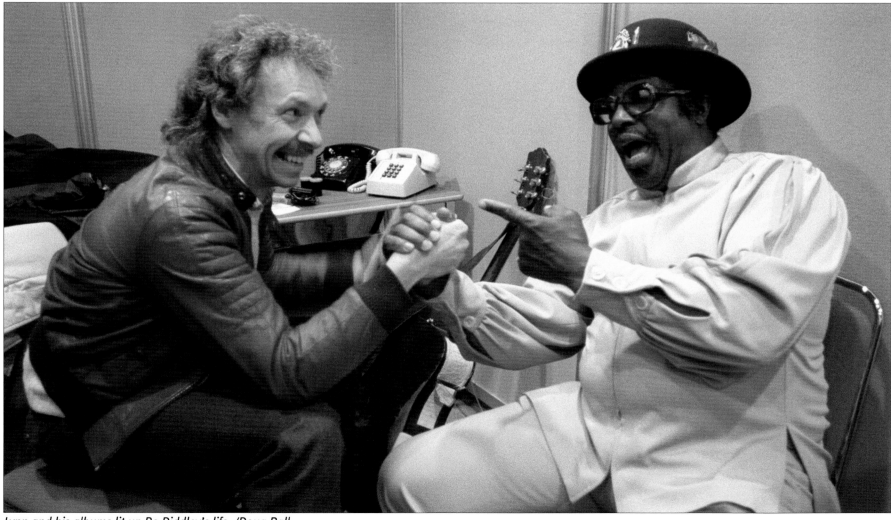

Lynn and his albums lit up Bo Diddley's life. /Doug Ball

A giant amaryllis dominates Mordecai Richler's kitchen table. Lynn thought he was an arrogant grump. /Lynn Ball, Ottawa Citizen

What am I, chopped liver?

By Lynn Ball

The roads were icy but I made it safely to Mordecai Richler's house on Lake Memphremagog in Quebec's Eastern Townships in January 1991. I was looking forward to meeting the famous writer for the first time. I did enjoy his work, especially *The Apprenticeship of Duddy Kravitz*.

Richler was in the kitchen chopping chicken livers. A large amaryllis flower on the counter leaned in as *Citizen* reporter Charles Lewis prodded a grumpy Mordecai with questions. I shot pictures. He made us coffee. When the chicken liver ritual was completed, I asked him for some shots at his pool table.

The low winter sun streaming over the frozen lake lit the room like a photographer's studio. Out of sorts, Mordecai refused to play along. I

Richler grudgingly agreed to pose for pool shots. /Lynn Ball, Ottawa Citizen

pleaded, saying I needed more than just him chopping liver. He co-operated eventually, but not for long.

Richler surprised me. My impression was of a miserable old man full of himself. We met again a short time later in the pressroom at a political convention in Ottawa. I said hello and re-introduced myself. He just grunted, then turned and walked away.

Hillary Clinton excited over a beavertail, an Ottawa Winterlude delicacy. Opposite page: Top, what Lynn saw as he skated backwards; bottom, what security saw as Lynn skated towards them. /Lynn Ball, Ottawa Citizen; John Major, Ottawa Citizen

First Lady's First Beavertail

By Lynn Ball

Most news photographers will bend over backwards for a Page One picture. Me, I skated backwards on the Rideau Canal during the annual Winterlude festival to catch Hillary Clinton munching a famous-in-Ottawa, doughnut-like delicacy called a Beavertail.

It was Saturday, Feb. 25, 1995, during U.S. President Bill Clinton and Mrs. Clinton's only official visit to Canada's capital city. According to the itinerary put out by the Prime Minister's Office, the First Lady was to skate along the Rideau Canal from Patterson Creek to Fifth Avenue to have lunch with her husband at the Canal Ritz restaurant – a distance of about half a kilometre. There was a media photographers' position set up at Fifth Avenue, complete with red carpeting to stand on.

Rather than settle for a routine shot with the pack, I laced on my hockey skates and headed for Patterson Creek, hoping to skate side-by-side with Hillary. But security spotted my press credentials dangling from my neck and gave me the boot. The public, out in the thousands for the winter carnival on the world's longest skating rink, was welcome to skate with the Clinton entourage, but not the press. So I slipped the accreditation badges into my pocket and instantly became a member of the public. Then I skated back to Patterson Creek and to Hillary.

I skated backwards in front of them as they approached Fifth Avenue, much to the fury of Secret Service agents skating on Hillary's flanks, who quickly realized that I was a member of the media. They couldn't catch me, even when I caught a skate in a crack and nearly went down. Then I heard a roar from the photographers set up on the Fifth Avenue stand – I was blocking their shot.

As they were cursing me, Hillary skated over to the Beavertails concession hut and was given one of the sugary treats. I was the only press photographer to catch her in mid-bite.

The passing of the torch: From Rocket Richard to Jean Beliveau (this page), from Henri Richard to Yvan Cournoyer, next page, then Canadiens leave the Forum ice for the last time. /Doug Ball

Passing the Torch at the Montreal Forum

By Doug Ball

Some events can make even a hard-bitten news photographer cry.

I played hockey growing up and in Australia in 1969 and in France in 1973. My boyhood hero was Gordie Howe of the Detroit Red Wings, my favourite team as well. When I moved to Montreal later in 1973 to join *The Canadian Press* news co-operative, it took me less than a year to become a Habs fan. I hated it when Montreal played Detroit.

In the summer of 1987, we moved from Montreal to Oakville, Ont. My great friend Chris Haney had enlisted me to help him build a golf course in Caledon called the Devil's Pulpit.

One day it was announced that the Montreal Canadiens were going to build a new arena and my beloved Montreal Forum would be no more. I dreaded the event, but on March 11, 1996, I headed to Montreal for the last game with a buddy, Bob Schneider. I had lined up two press passes.

The game was so-so, a Habs 4-1 victory over the Dallas Stars. But the ceremony to mark the closing of the Forum was spectacular. Thanks to our press passes, Schneider and I were on the ice right up against the penalty box with a clear view of the walkway where the dignitaries would appear.

The Montreal Canadiens' players in the Hockey Hall of Fame were standing on a large rectangular red carpet. Habs' oldest living captain Butch Bouchard walked onto the ice from the dressing room carrying a torch. In the Habs' dressing room a line of John McCrae's poem *In Flanders Fields* was mounted on the wall. *...To you from failing hands we throw the torch; be yours to hold it high.*

That did it. I was crying. Even the seven-minute ovation for Rocket Richard didn't bother me. Then Bouchard walked over and passed the torch to The Rocket, then Rocket to Jean Beliveau. Beliveau walked past Dickie Moore and passed the flame to Henri Richard. Moore was passed up as only a team captain can carry the torch.

I got every pass of the torch on film but I really like the one of The Rocket passing it to Jean Beliveau.

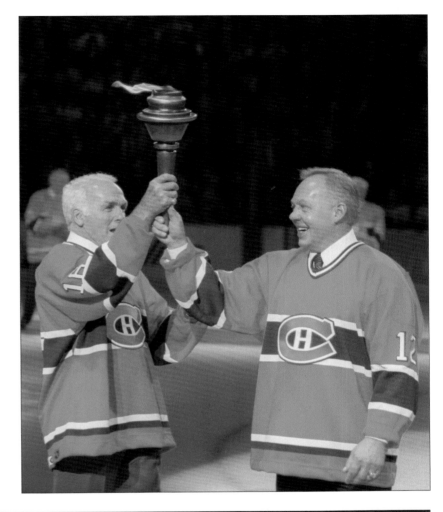

Kermit "Shine" Forbes, who sparred with Ernest Hemingway, loved to show off his mementos in and around his Key West home. /Lynn Ball, Ottawa Citizen

Sparring with Ernest Hemingway

By Lynn Ball

Kermit "Shine" Forbes found a lifetime of fame and friendship for throwing a punch at Ernest Hemingway. When we met, Shine was 82. The event that made his name had taken place 60 years earlier.

In Florida, in March 1998, to cover Montreal Expos and Ottawa Lynx spring training camp for *The Ottawa Citizen*, I made a side trip to take some feature pictures for stories by *Citizen* writer Janice Kennedy. One was about "Papa" Hemingway's sparring partner, Shine.

As we meandered from Shine's home on one of Key West's back alleys to Hemingway's house to take some photos, there was a steady stream of greetings and waves. We stopped for a drink. The bartender gave him a beer. I met his barber and was introduced to friends who ran a bakeshop. He pointed out all the good watering holes and a couple of places that used to be "cat houses". "I spent many a night in there," Shine said.

One night, the young fighter was a corner man for a friend in a boxing match. Hemingway was the referee. With no inkling of who Hemingway was, Shine figured the man was refereeing simply for beer money.

Shine's friend was getting beaten badly so Shine threw in the towel to end the fight. The referee threw it out. Shine threw it back in. The referee threw it out again. Shine tried once more to end it. This time, Hemingway pitched the towel right in Shine's face.

"So I jumps in the ring and took a poke at him."

Hemingway grabbed Shine by the ear and then everyone got into the ring including the constable who asked Hemingway if he wanted Shine to be put in jail.

"No," the famous writer said. "Anyone with the guts to take a poke at me shouldn't go to jail."

After Shine found out he'd taken a poke at Ernest Hemingway he went around to apologize.

Shine was in his early 20s and Hemingway in his late 30s when Shine took his punch at him. That punch changed Shine's life. He and his buddies, "Iron Baby" and "Black Pie", began training and boxing at Hemingway's place. They would fight three rounds each against Hemingway with Shine going last. Hemingway was six feet tall and weighed over 200 pounds while Shine was 5'6" and 135 pounds.

My visit to the old boxer's home was unforgettable. "Shine's Pondarosa (sic)" was in part of a long-gone dairy, the outside was a clutter of artifi-

cial flowers, statues, carvings, flags and other bits and pieces covering the sidewalk, plants and a palm tree by his front door.

Wearing a ball cap with Canada geese and Canada embroidered on it, my host showed me around. The bed was to the right just inside the door and a small kitchen on the left. There wasn't a bit of wall or ceiling that didn't have a picture, artifact or religious icon stuck to it or hung from it. Some of the photographs were of Shine with famous boxers and movie stars.

Two of the biggest pictures he had pinned up side by side, his prize possessions, Hemingway in a boxer's pose and Shine the boxer.

Shine died in 2000.

Slugging It Out with Big Mac

By Lynn Ball

Not all the fans of baseball heroes are in the stands. Sometimes they're playing right on the field with them.

I was assigned to cover the Montreal Expos and the Ottawa Lynx spring training camp in 1998, the year the Expos began spring training in Jupiter, Fla., sharing their new facilities with the St. Louis Cardinals.

I wanted to see slugger Mark McGwire hit a few over the fence so I hung around one day after the Expos had finished to watch the Cardinals practise. I had seen McGwire play with Oakland when they defeated the Toronto Blue Jays in the American League playoffs in the early '90s and I couldn't resist leaning against the batting cage and at close range watch McGwire whack some balls out of the park. It was one of the perks of a press pass.

Expos' F. P. Santangelo stayed out to watch Big Mac and we were standing next to each other outside the batting cage. When McGwire ended practice and was leaving the cage, Santangelo turned to me, "I'm going to ask him for his bat," he said, and headed around the cage to intercept McGwire.

I followed and took pictures. McGwire handed over his bat at Santangelo's request and they talked a bit. As they parted, McGwire, instead of shaking hands, thumped Santangelo on the chest twice with his mighty fist.

Santangelo came back with the bat in hand and a huge grin.

"Maybe there's a few homers in it for you, Santangelo?" I suggested.

"No. It's going in the case at home."

That summer, McGwire set a single season home run record with 70 homers. Santangelo hit a total of 21 home runs in his seven-year career. Maybe he should have used McGwire's bat.

Slugger Mark McGwire thumps his fist on the chest of F. P. Santangelo. /Lynn Ball, Ottawa Citizen

A Faceful of Pepper Spray

By Lynn Ball

"Why aren't you at the demo on the Hill?" photo assignment editor Anita Murray inquired as I walked into *The Ottawa Citizen* newsroom to file the pictures from my day's assignments.

"What demo?"

"Oh, I forgot to tell you," Anita said.

It was already past 1 p.m. on a cold Nov. 18, 1999, by the time I got downtown to Parliament Hill. In a national day of action against homelessness, the Ontario Coalition Against Poverty had bused in marchers from Toronto, Kingston, Montreal and the Tyendinaga Mohawk community near Belleville.

The Toronto-based OCAP, protesting the federal budget, had the support of The Canadian Union of Postal Workers, the Comité des san-emplois and the Canadian Labour Congress. About 250 protesters assembled in the Byward Market at noon for their march. The anti-poverty groups wanted payment increases to employment insurance, welfare and child credits and a doubling of the federal budget for social housing.

The marchers were passing the West Block when I arrived and moved towards the Centre Block where the RCMP in fur hats, assisted by the Ottawa city police, had lined up behind steel barricades several metres in front of the main entrances. I cut across the lawn between the law and the demonstrators to intercept them.

What I didn't know was that they had come to fight, not demonstrate. When they got about six metres away from the police, they charged and I was caught in the middle. They got to the barricades and tried to push them over, but the police responded with pepper spray. It worked. The charge quickly turned into retreat.

Unfortunately, I got a face full of pepper spray.

It was in my eyes, up my nose and in my mouth but I did get a good picture out of it. Just before the effects of the pepper spray took me out, I got a shot of a protester screaming, his hand in the air in an attempt to stop the pepper spray shot into his face by a determined police officer.

The protesters were prepared for the assault and had bottles of water waiting to wash the noxious liquid from their eyes and noses. When they could see again, they rallied for a second charge, towels and sweaters wrapped around their faces.

The riot police were ready, replacing fur hats with hard hats and face shields. The lipstick-sized pepper sprayers were exchanged for pepper sprayers the size of fire extinguishers.

The protesters charged again and threw the steel barricades into the air. I looked up and there was a barricade over me. I backed off quickly. I still don't know why the flying steel barricades injured no one.

Some of the protesters had hockey sticks with the blades cut off which they swung at the police. The rear guard threw the sticks like spears while others pitched cans of food.

The large canisters of pepper spray soon did the trick and another retreat was on. Out of ammunition for another assault, the activists left the Hill.

These were nothing but hooligans itching for a fight with police and didn't do much good for their cause. During the second assault, I kept my left eye shut and held my camera hard against my right eye to keep the spray out. It sort of worked. I still got hit by stinging liquid but I survived to shoot the pictures.

During the civil rights days in Alabama when I was with Martin Luther King, I learned that "the man with the stick is always right". These protesters found this out.

Photographers, like demonstrators, run the risk of getting pepper sprayed. /Lynn Ball, Ottawa Citizen

In the last game at Maple Leaf Gardens, Chicago beat Toronto 6-2. /Doug Ball

1998-99 SEASON
PHOTOGRAPHER PASS
TORONTO MAPLE LEAFS
1931-1999
MAPLE LEAF GARDENS
MEMORIES & DREAMS
FEBRUARY 13, 1999
ISSUED TO: Doug Ball
AFFILIATION: Chicago Tribune

1998-99 SEASON
PHOTOGRAPHER PASS
TORONTO MAPLE LEAFS
1931-1999
MAPLE LEAF GARDENS
MEMORIES & DREAMS
FEBRUARY 13, 1999
ISSUED TO: Lynn Ball
AFFILIATION: National Post
PHOTOGRAPHER PASS
ACCESS TO:
MEDIA ROOM &
DRESSING ROOMS

The Night the Leafs Played like Honky the Christmas Goose

By Lynn Ball

The last game at Maple Leaf Gardens was to take place Feb. 13, 1999, the Toronto Maple Leafs against the Chicago Blackhawks, and I wanted to be there. I had been turned down for a press pass to represent *The Ottawa Citizen*, so I called Hans Deryk at *The National Post*. He had three passes but was sending just two photographers. I was in luck.

At the Gardens' entrance, I met brother Doug, who had arranged for a pass from *The Chicago Tribune*, and we picked up our passes and went to the pressroom. I had my 1965 Stanley Cup playoff pass and wore it with my game pass. People noticed it and I was asked several times if I wanted to sell it. I finally had to take off the old pass as I thought a rabid fan, wanting to add it to his Maple Leaf Gardens memorabilia collection, might mug me.

The special programs went on sale and it was a free-for-all as mobs attacked the program sellers. The souvenir programs came in a sealed plastic bag. I had some pictures in it so I wanted one to keep unopened in pristine collectable condition. I managed to get three, one for my friend Brian Logie and two for me.

The game sure wasn't like the ones I had covered at the Gardens in the mid-'60s. The Leafs sucked, the Blackhawks made monkeys of the defence and Toronto was soundly beaten 6-2. Hawks tough guy Bob Probert scored the last NHL goal in the Gardens. It was his second goal of the night.

The rest of night was great; Ron MacLean wearing a top hat, Stompin' Tom Connors, Anne Murray; what a show. Most of the old Leafs were there and were introduced to wild cheers, especially Eddie Shack.

After the game, the retired Leaf players walked back onto the ice for one last feel of the Gardens. Doug and I walked onto the ice as well. Brad Marsh was getting other players to sign his sweater. Johnny Bower and

Eddie Shack were both singing Bower's hit song *Honky the Christmas Goose*. Then they sang Eddie's song, a hit in Toronto in the '60s, *Clear the Track, Here Comes Shack*. Toronto enforcer Tie Domi gathered a group of his favourite Leafs together for a picture.

Slowly everyone drifted off the ice and Maple Leaf Gardens was silent and empty.

Retired Leaf greats on the ice, above; below, TV commentator Ron MacLean in fine form and Curtis Joseph letting in the last goal at Maple Leaf Gardens. Lynn Ball, Ottawa Citizen

An old motorized Nikon F captured this moment of Gretzky's solitary glory. /Lynn Ball, Ottawa Citizen

Old Cameras neither Die nor Lose Their Focus

By Lynn Ball

I had heard that Wayne Gretzky was going to announce his retirement in New York at the New York Rangers' last game of the year, April 18, 1999. The Rangers' second-last game was in Ottawa a few days before on April 15, so I knew it would be his last game in Canada.

This was going to be an historic event and I wanted to be there. I was still using film to take my pictures and *The Ottawa Citizen* rules were such that only photographers with digital cameras could cover hockey games.

However, the newspaper had three passes for the Corel Centre that night and assigned just two photographers to cover the event. I asked for the remaining pass.

I said, "Anything I shoot, you can have."

It was sort of an uninspired game overall and I concentrated on Gretzky most of the time. Nothing of historic proportions was happening. With 4:43 left in the third period, a television time out was called and all of the players went to their respective benches.

When the play would resume, the face-off would be right in front of me.

The crowd began to chant. "ONE MORE YEAR. . . ONE MORE YEAR. . . ONE MORE YEAR." Gretzky skated from his bench to where the face-off would be. The chants grew louder.

Gretzky gave small waves indicating they should stop but the fans wouldn't stop. He circled in front of me and I could see a tear in his eye but it was something that wouldn't show up in a photograph.

The marquee that surrounds the rink suddenly lit up with "THE GREAT ONE ... WAYNE GRETZKY #99."

I couldn't believe it! If only Gretzky would get into position so that I could get this in a picture.

"Stay on the bench. Stay on the bench," I kept saying in my head to the other players. They did. They were all enjoying the moment, watching The Great One. Then Gretzky skated away from me and turned raising his stick in a salute to the fans.

I stuck my old motorized Nikon F with a pre-focused 35 mm 2.8 lens through the hole in the glass and let a burst of the motor go. Then I picked up my gear and headed for the door and *The Citizen's* darkroom.

I had the picture of Wayne Gretzky that captured the historic moment of his last game in Canada. There he was framed in a salute to the fans with the sign THE GREAT ONE ... WAYNE GRETZKY #99 above him.

My picture, taken with a 40-year-old camera, ran the full width of the front page.

The Citizen did all right, too. Prints sold by the hundreds.

Most photos shot from the back don't work out – except in moments like this. /Doug Ball

The Great One's Last Game

By Doug Ball

I've always been a hockey fan. When I was working for *The Canadian Press* in Toronto, I covered the Maple Leafs. At *CP* in Montreal, I covered the Habs and just loved it.

In the '90s, I took time off work to attend the final games at three of the original six arenas, Chicago Stadium, Maple Leaf Gardens and the Montreal Forum.

When I heard that Wayne Gretzky was doing his final tour of arenas, I tried to figure out a way to get into Madison Square Garden to shoot his last New York game, April 18, 1999.

I had worked part time for *The Toronto Star* in the late '80s, so I called to find out if they were sending a photographer to New York for Gretzky's last game. They weren't so I asked them to put my name in for a media pass at the New York Rangers media office. They did.

During the week before the event, I called the Rangers' public relations people. The guy was very nice but said he wasn't sure I could cover the game because there were four holes in the glass at each corner of the rink and there were 16 photographers already accredited. But he didn't say I couldn't come.

On Saturday before Sunday's big game, I drove from Toronto to Woodstock, N.Y., and spent the night. *("Thought I'd join a rock and roll band. Camp out on the land and try to set my soul free.")* I drove into Manhattan late Sunday morning, parked the car and went to the media entrance of Madison Square Garden. There was a long line of journalists waiting to get their passes. I joined in and ran into a number of old friends. Eventually I was at the front of the line.

"Doug Ball, *Toronto Star*," I said, expecting nothing. A girl whipped out an envelope with my pass in it. Wow, even the pass was a keeper!

The pre-game ceremony was well done. Gretzky's dad, Walter, came out on the ice in a new Mercedes Benz, a gift from the Rangers' organization. His wife, Janet, and the Rangers' captain and assistants, and Mark Messier and Mario Lemieux, joined Gretzky on the ice.

It was game time. I went up to a hallway above the ice and talked to an usher. He let me stay there even though he wasn't supposed to. I think he felt sorry for me having driven all the way from Toronto. Just before the end of the game, I dug into my camera bag and pulled out a present for the guy. It was a hat from the Masters golf tournament that I had covered the previous week. He was speechless and that's tough for a New Yorker.

At the end of the game, nobody wanted it to end. All of the photographers went on to the ice to get a shot of Gretzky making his endless number of last laps. One of the photos I took of the hockey giant from the back with a 6X9 Fuji camera turned out great. A spotlighted Gretzky waving, sweater tucked in and hats landing on the ice.

The Toronto Star ran it full page in a special section on Gretzky when he was inducted into the Hockey Hall of Fame.

An ancient Leica film camera captured the departure of Trudeau's casket from Parliament Hill. /Lynn Ball, Ottawa Citizen

Shooting Bold with the Old

By Lynn Ball

I love vintage cars and vintage cameras. Sometimes they can knock the stuffing out of newfangled contraptions.

On Oct. 2, 2000, Pierre Trudeau's body was taken from the Centre Block of the Parliament Buildings in Ottawa and transported by train to Montreal for his funeral. I was assigned to cover this event by *The Ottawa Citizen*. It was the era of digital cameras but I didn't have one. I was using a 1967 Nikon F and my museum-piece 1950 Leica 111F.

When the casket carried by the RCMP pallbearers descended the steps of the Centre Block, Trudeau's sons Justin and Alexandre (Sasha), appeared behind it.

I shot a vertical photo when it was framed the way I wanted with my old Leica. The camera isn't motorized so it was a one shot deal.

After the funeral cars left the Hill, I got a call on my cell phone. The city desk was watching the event live on television and Margaret Trudeau was talking with people near the Centennial Flame.

Citizen photographer Rod MacIvor was there as well and I told him about Margaret and we both went down to the flame. Rod and I kept our distance. I took a few shots of her with a telephoto lens. Suddenly, we saw her break down in tears and start to run from the crowd.

Then she spotted Rod. Rod knows her quite well as he'd taught her photography years earlier. Margaret, very distraught, ran up and put her arms around him, crying. Rod helped settle her down and some friends came up and took her away.

Back at *The Citizen*, photo editor Drew Gragg came up to me and said, "Great photo from The Hill, we're using it full page tomorrow. By the way, what did you shoot it with?"

I held up my old Leica.

"We've just spent $70,000 to equip each photographer with digital cameras and you get the best picture with an antique!"

The picture was used full page in colour in a special 14-page section titled PIERRE TRUDEAU.

Citizen photographer Rod MacIvor consoles Margaret Trudeau near the Centennial Flame. /Lynn Ball, Ottawa Citizen

Mike Weir receives the famous green jacket from Tiger Woods at the Masters Tournament in April 2003. /Doug Ball

Lucky 13 was a Masterful Shot

By Doug Ball

It's tough to get a photo pass for the U.S. Masters. News wire services like *The Associated Press* and *Reuters* get just two coveted passes each.

Augusta is the only golf tournament I've covered where photographers are not allowed inside the ropes so they can move from hole to hole with the leaders. That makes it a tough event to photograph.

In 1997, without a ticket or photo pass, I stayed in a rented house with sports writers Cam Cole of *The National Post*, Ken Fidlin of *The Toronto Sun* and Dave Perkins of *The Toronto Star*.

The Star picked up the cost of the house as I had done some free-lance work earlier. I also cooked for the three scribes. I was waiting and hoping that I would get a pass from someone leaving early on Sunday.

One afternoon, I was sitting at the bar at the French Market Grill West with two other people – the barmaid, who was counting her lunch receipts, and a big guy a few stools away. We watched the Masters on television and chatted.

The big guy was Ron Harrison, who was in real estate and also dealt in the sale and transfer of Masters' tickets. He said he had arranged for 30 tickets for a large U.S. company bringing a lot of their clients to Georgia for the week. Some played golf at nearby courses and others went to the Masters for the day. Harrison had a van parked across the street from Gate 4 on Washington Road and some reserved parking spots.

The clients would report to him in the van and he would mark down the number on the ticket before passing it to them. That day in the bar, Harrison said I could get in every day with his tickets as some clients would stay just a few hours to watch golf and turn their tickets back in and leave. If I showed up around 1 p.m. every day I could probably get in. He was right.

After meeting Harrison, I went down to the Masters every year. Then, for the first time in a long time, in April 2003, I decided not to go down to Georgia. The winter before, Harrison had passed away from a heart attack. I didn't know who was going to do the job for him and after five years of visiting with Ron, it wasn't going to be the same.

So, I was at home watching the Masters on TV when Canadian Mike Weir climbed to the top of the heap with one round to go. I decided it was time for me to go.

I phoned a friend, Ed Wilson, and asked him what he was doing.

"When are we leaving?" he asked.

"15 minutes," I said.

I was supposed to be picking up an old friend in New York arriving from Southampton on the *Queen Elizabeth II* in his car, a nice Mercedes that I had just had serviced that week. I figured he wouldn't mind if I took the car. I didn't have time to ask.

We left Oakville, Ont., at 6 p.m. on Saturday and drove straight through to Augusta, 13 hours exactly. We called a buddy, Dan Walshe with *TSN*, who had rented a house for the week and went over and had a three-hour nap.

Then we headed down to see if the van was parked in the same place across from Gate 4 on Washington Road.

It was. Ron's friend, Norman, was standing in but couldn't help us. No tickets available.

We spent a couple of hours at Hooters before deciding to try again. This time Norman had a handful of tickets.

"Could we have a couple?"

"No problem."

Now the problem was how to get a camera in undetected. I took off the lens and put it in the pocket of my windbreaker. I slung the camera body over my shoulder under the jacket. It was a little warm for a windbreaker but it did the trick.

I knew a lot of the photographers covering the event but I kept the camera hidden until Mike Weir won his green jacket. All of the photographers would be going to the practice green for the official ceremony to see him receive it from Tiger Woods. A roped-off area was reserved just for us.

I waited until all of the photogs were running to get a good spot. I took out my camera to look professional and ran with them. The guard didn't ask for my pass because he thought I was one of them. I was in the photo pool undetected, home free.

My friend Ed watched on the patrons' side of the ropes.

When it was over, we made our way back to Norman in the van and returned the tickets along with a crisp $50 U.S.

It was 8 p.m. and we pointed the Mercedes north, 1-20, 1-77, 47, I-79, I-90 and the QEW. We were back. It's 9 a.m. on Monday. Ed heads straight on to work. We had 13 hours down, 13 hours there and 13 hours home.

Lucky 13 got me one of my favourite photos of all time.

Mike Weir, 32, became the first Canadian to win a Major and the first left-hander to take the U.S. Masters.

Tiger Woods winning the Masters in 1997. /Doug Ball

Kim Campbell's Short Term

Prime Minister Kim Campbell, in office from June 25 to Nov. 3, 1993, talks to the media outside Rideau Hall in Ottawa on Sept. 8, 1993 after a visit with Governor General Ray Hnatyshyn to call an election for Oct. 25. The election gutted the Progressive Conservatives, reducing the party to two seats. It never recovered, eventually merging with the Alliance Party to form a new Conservative Party.
Lynn Ball, Ottawa Citizen

Listen up, Jean

Eugene Whelan has Jean Chretien's attention as he whispers to him at a breakfast meeting during the Liberal leadership campaign at an Ottawa hotel in March 1990. It must have been good advice as Chretien won his leadership bid to become prime minister. */Lynn Ball, Ottawa Citizen*

Arnold Palmer's Last British Open

Being a bit of a golf nut — I've only missed two British Opens since 1983 — I wasn't looking forward to the 1990 championship because it might be Arnold Palmer's last kick at the can. He had won the 1961 and 1962 Opens and the rules stated the past champions are exempt from qualifying up to the age of 65. Palmer would be 65 a few months before the next Open at St. Andrews in 1995. So I got a photo of him driving off the 18th hole and thought that would be his last.

Luckily, the Royal and Ancient realized what importance he had for the game so they changed the rules for exemptions for past champions to read 65 and under. They wanted him to play in the 1995 Open and wave goodbye on the bridge.

He did it perfectly. He was going to miss the cut on Friday so the photographers had planned a special event to get a shot of him waving goodbye with the R&A building in the background. Then he parred the hole and went into the scoring tent to sign his final card.

I followed him to the media tent for his last news conference when a woman stopped him and asked him if, on the occasion, would he like a drink of the champagne she was holding. Palmer, always knowing where he was, said "No thank you ma'am, but I wouldn't mind a scotch and water." He drank it all through his conference. One American journalist asked what kind of scotch it was and the press officer quickly said, " I'm sorry sir, that wouldn't be fair."

— By Doug Ball

Doug Ball, Canadian Press

Gary Carter and the Howler

At the Montreal Expos spring training camp in West Palm Beach, Fla., in March 1981, a young couple and their baby from Montreal approached Expos star catcher Gary Carter. They asked him to hold their son, dressed in a miniature ball player's uniform, while they took a picture. Carter agreed and they handed over the tot, who started instantly to howl in his loudest voice. Startling and unforeseen, the situation made a good picture running Page One back in Ottawa. Many years later, at the Expos spring training camp in 1998, I asked Carter if he remembered the incident. "Yeah," he said with a laugh, "That kid really screamed." – *Lynn Ball*

Lynn Ball, Ottawa Citizen

Blowin' in the Wind

In a snapshot straight out of *Life*, Ken Huckabone of Renfrew, Ont., takes his dog for a ride on his motorcycle in the 1960s. I stopped him and asked why the kerchief. He said the dachshund loved riding on the bike but didn't like the wind in her ears. The photo ran in *The Star Weekly*, a popular weekend magazine published at that time by *The Toronto Star*. – *Lynn Ball*

Lynn Ball, Ottawa Citizen

Soul Legend in Town

On July 13, 2001, Godfather of Soul James Brown performed before a record crowd of 27,000 at the LeBreton Flats site of the Ottawa Bluesfest. "He came out on the good foot and just got better and better. By the time it came to do Sex Machine, his 25-minute marathon, the crowd was in the palm of the man's hand," The *Ottawa Citizen* wrote. The next day, anxious to blow this town, he wasn't interested in talking or posing. Then, Lynn Ball arrives calling out, "Reverend Cleophus," Brown's character's name in *The Blues Brothers* movie. "Do you know that?" Brown asks Ball. "It's my favourite movie," replies Ball. Without any prompting, Brown recites his famous line, "Do you see the light? Do you see the light?" And, in his best Reverend Cleophus stance, with his fingers pointing in mid-air, James Brown pauses for a moment while Lynn Ball snaps his picture.
– *Tony Lofaro*

Lynn Ball, Ottawa Citizen

Pipers Scattered for the Exits

At the annual Glengarry Highland Games in Maxville, Ont., on a mid-summer Friday evening in 1974 the sky cracked open and hell broke loose. Massed bands were playing in front of the grandstand as a massive black thundercloud moved towards us with large bolts of lightning. As the thunder banged and roared, I set my camera at 1/30 of a second, hoping, if my reflexes were fast enough, to catch a lightning shot. A bolt struck just behind the pipe band and I took a shot. I got it! Then it began to pour. Without an order to break ranks, the pipers and drummers ran for cover. I got soaked but I got some great pictures, kilts flying up and pipers scattering. This is a print of one of my favourite pictures from that wild evening. A drummer walks through water with a bass drum on his head for protection from the rain.
–Lynn Ball

Lynn Ball, Ottawa Citizen

My $1,000 Blue Heron

By Lynn Ball

Some pictures are worth a thousand words. This one was worth a thousand dollars. In July 1979, I moved to my 260-hectare (650 acres) farm near the historic Ontario town of Merrickville, an hour's drive southwest of Ottawa. One morning in early September on my way to work I saw a great blue heron. The majestic bird, the largest of the North American herons and egrets, stood four feet tall in the water just below the Rideau River dam in Merrickville, the sun sparkling off the water.

I stopped the car and got out to take a photograph but the bird took off before I had the chance. It didn't fly far and when it landed the heron was in the midst of a mist. It was a beautiful scene and I thought it would be a good picture for the final edition of *The Ottawa Citizen*. The editors liked something fresh for the afternoon home-delivered evening paper.

Managing editor Nelson Skuce liked the heron so much he said we would save it for the next day and run it in all editions on Page One.

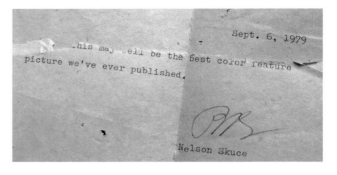

The response was overwhelming. Calls for reprints clogged *The Citizen's* switchboard for three weeks. Some people ordered it enlarged to 30 by 40 inches.

Skuce wrote me a note saying it was the best colour feature photograph *The Citizen* had ever published. The paper made so much money selling reprints they gave me a $1,000 bonus. I guess the heron knew it didn't look good where I first spotted it so it flew to a better place to be photographed. That heron sure had an eye for pictures.

Lynn Ball's $1,000 heron amid the mists of the Rideau. /Lynn Ball, Ottawa Citizen

AND IN THE END...

Well, that's done!
I have been thinking of this book for about 10 years and it's too bad
our dad couldn't see it. I am still doing some freelance photography
but with little or no pressure like the old wire service days. And I've
found a little bit of heaven in Caledon, northwest of Toronto, where I
play a lot of golf at the Devil's Pulpit.
– *Doug Ball*

After 45 years working as a photographer, 32 of them as chief photographer at *The Ottawa Citizen*, I retired in August 2003. People asked, "What are you going to do when you retire?" I replied, "What I want, when I want." I now have time to enjoy the country life and my vegetable garden on my farm near Eastons Corners in Eastern Ontario, more time troutin', salmon fishing, hiking and relaxing at the cottage in Salvage, Nfld., canoeing and camping in Algonquin Park, hot rodding in the Corvettes and slowly restoring a Lotus 30 race car. I also do a little bit of freelance photography. I highly recommend retirement.
– *Lynn Ball*

•

Before their careers in photography blossomed, Lynn and Doug drove a 1962
Corvette around the world. Here in Queensland, Australia, in October 1969, the
brothers were on their way to Rubyvale to prospect and mine sapphires. A water-
bag hangs from the front bumper and surfboards rest on a rack. They have enough
material from the trip to write a book. And maybe they will.

Index

Index

Index